A CALL TO THE VILLAGE

Retooling Public Schools

Wana L. Duhart

Rowman & Littlefield Education
Lanham, Maryland • Toronto • Plymouth, UK
2007

Published in the United States of America
by Rowman & Littlefield Education
A Division of Rowman & Littlefield Publishers, Inc.
A wholly owned subsidiary of The Rowman & Littlefield Publishing Group, Inc.
4501 Forbes Boulevard, Suite 200, Lanham, Maryland 20706
www.rowmaneducation.com

Estover Road
Plymouth PL6 7PY
United Kingdom

Copyright © 2007 by Wana L. Duhart

All rights reserved. No part of this publication may be reproduced, stored in a retrieval system, or transmitted in any form or by any means, electronic, mechanical, photocopying, recording, or otherwise, without the prior permission of the publisher.

British Library Cataloguing in Publication Information Available

Library of Congress Cataloging-in-Publication Data

Duhart, Wana L., 1963–
  A call to the village : retooling public schools / Wana L. Duhart.
    p. cm.
  ISBN-13: 978-1-57886-634-2 (hardback : alk. paper)
  ISBN-13: 978-1-57886-635-9 (pbk. : alk. paper)
  ISBN-10: 1-57886-634-0 (hardback : alk. paper)
  ISBN-10: 1-57886-635-9 (pbk. : alk. paper)
  1. Public schools—United States. 2. Educational change—United States. 3. Public-private sector cooperation—United States. 4. Community and school—United States. I. Title.
  LA217.2.D84 2007
  371.010973—dc22
                                                              2007011517

∞™ The paper used in this publication meets the minimum requirements of American National Standard for Information Sciences—Permanence of Paper for Printed Library Materials, ANSI/NISO Z39.48-1992.
Manufactured in the United States of America.

For my mother

CONTENTS

Preface		vii
Introduction to Cross-Sectoral Collaboration		xv
1	The Paradigm Shift in Elementary and Secondary Education	1
2	Strategic Alternatives: Market- Versus System-Based Reform	15
3	Benefits of Cross-Sectoral Collaboration	39
4	Implementation Challenges and Realities	57
5	Beyond the Walls of the "Church"	77
6	The Prominence of the Nonprofit Community	91
7	Maximizing Stakeholder Value in Education	103
8	The Quandary of the Public Sector	119
9	Concluding Thoughts	131

PREFACE

A CALL TO THE VILLAGE

Many of us feel a sense of passion about elementary and secondary education because we bear witness to how important a role it has played in our own lives as we developed and matured into adulthood. Although some of us learned during our early school years that we had certain intellectual, artistic, or athletic abilities, others gained the self-confidence needed to continue their chosen paths in life. Similarly, just as some developed an appreciation for classmates who had different life experiences, there were those who simply learned discipline and order for the first time in their lives because of classroom structure. These tangible and intangible benefits that many gained while in grade school explain why so many people from all walks of life are compelled to participate in improving public schools. We happen to believe that the magic that occurred for us during those early years can be restored for today's youth.

In some ways, it is amazing to witness the range of reform initiatives being implemented across the country. But then again, it is not so amazing, because public schools laid a strong foundation for so many people across so many communities for decades. The breadth and volume of contributions are not only a testament to people's personal commitment to public schools but also a revelation about their willingness to reach back and try to re-create educational opportunities for school-age children in today's society. The creation of scholarship programs to encourage young people to succeed throughout their early grades has been effective in some communities. The opening of new school prototypes to address identifiable student needs in certain markets has proven to be a timely means of intervention. As entities representing many professions, industries, and sectors increasingly engage in the school reform movement, the range of solutions to local school dilemmas will widen and ultimately reflect both the uniqueness and the complexity of the problems in education.

As a product of public schools, I am convinced that they can work once again. I believe that schools can be retooled to produce academically prepared students for a changed and global world. Because markets, industries, and cultures were less interdependent decades ago, academic training at the elementary and secondary levels did not need to be as cross-disciplinary and integrated, as is necessary in this millennium. The predictability and simplicity of the past that allowed school-age education to be conducted by teaching subjects isolated from existing realities are long gone. Our complex and uncertain world demands education formats that draw on relationships between academia and praxis. The old static and passive ways of teaching and learning have been replaced with more dynamic and integrative approaches, characterized by improved student–teacher dialogue and exchange.

The causes and effects of the disarray throughout the school systems are elusive and not always apparent. The systemic weaknesses of schools have been masked for years by Band-Aid remedies and quick fixes that were never intended to correct inherent problems in the systems and structures. For example, as educators continued to track students into groups and channel those deemed difficult to teach into special education, they failed to understand that learning differences and challenges did not equate to a child's inability to learn but was an indication that a child's learning style required a different teaching approach. Although the effects of the failures to adequately address the problems were not readily seen or felt for decades, the current state of schools and student achievement across the country is all the evidence that we need to understand that the decline has been gradual and is both massive and far reaching. The result of the complacency and disregard within the ranks of educators is a collage of public school systems nationwide that yield similar outcomes—a large percentage of youth who do not excel academically and are not equipped for postsecondary education and beyond.

Having spent almost two decades as a professional working in varied capacities across many sectors, I witnessed the diverse approaches being employed by individuals and institutions to display their concerns for failing schools. I began to envision professionals, industries, and sectors working together—that is, collaborating toward a common goal, which is the transformation of elementary and secondary schools in communities all across the nation. As an accounting and finance executive in the private sector, I developed an appreciation for measurable outcomes, clearly defined financial goals, organizational effectiveness, and efficiencies as salient priorities. Similarly, the important role that strategic philanthropy—especially, that in education—plays in the overall agendas of private companies and entrepreneurs always seemed to support the organizational priorities of maintaining competitiveness and ensuring longevity. My volunteer efforts and pro bono consulting work with nonprofits allowed me to witness how the nonprofit sector's work in bridging economic and social gaps was becoming critical for the sustainability and viability of neighborhoods and communities. The support and maintenance of community institutions such as schools were becoming a prominent aspect of nonprofit missions. As a theology student and local church officer, I gained a definite understanding of the religious sector's need to respond to the range of social and economic dilemmas confronting its parishioners on a daily basis. The ministerial pursuits of faith communities were extending beyond tradition to achieve a certain degree of relevance in surrounding communities.

A Call to the Village was born out of these experiences across the sectors. It is an opportunity for me to present a strategic road map that integrates the multiplicity of my experiences and utilizes my strategic, financial, analytical, and organizational skills. It is my attempt to build bridges across the sectors as a means of creating forums for persons and organizations to discover their roles in reforming local schools. By integrating the expertise of those who recognize different learning styles and paces, we can prevent thousands of gifted and talented young people from collapsing into oblivion. The fresh perspectives of participants from all sectors is critical to school-age learning, in part because it is the sectors that represent the environments in which most of our youth will work. Professionals and firms from across the sectors know best what knowledge and skills students will need to become successful leaders, citizens, managers, and workers.

The collaboration of parents, classroom teachers, policymakers, businesspeople, clerics, social service providers, foundations, concerned citizens, corporations, academics, and school administrators from all of the sectors represents infinite possibilities for reform locally and nationally. Indeed, the 500,000 organizations that make up the nonprofit sector can offer significant input into how local communities can better serve school-age youth. The financial and management expertise of private enterprise can elevate how public schools operate and manage their systems and resources. As a large majority of the 250,000 congregations nationwide expand their ministries to address public and social issues, their perspectives and influence become evermore vital for improving local schools. The contributions of these professionals from different sectors can work wonders in public education while making life in the classroom much more fulfilling for the 3 million elementary and secondary teaching professionals who compose a large segment of the public sector. The 100,000 public elementary and secondary schools and 50 million students nationwide are ample reasons for active participation by all sectors to assist in school reform.

Fixing our public schools is undoubtedly the preeminent domestic public policy challenge of this century. We must continue to move strategically toward an educational landscape that redefines, refines, and reengineers how elementary and secondary education is delivered to school-age youth in rural, suburban, and urban communities all across America. To be sure, the globalization of the marketplace and the information and technological explosion over the past few decades are sufficient evidence of the urgent need to transform schools so that youth are better prepared for an increasingly competitive and constantly changing world. The viable solutions for local schools are some combination of complete overhauls, innovative prototypes, higher standards, and greater accountability. Through collaboration, communities can develop clear strategies that incorporate some degree of each dimension. Young people are depending on us to develop formats and prototypes that will endow them with the tools and resources that they need to utilize their gifts and abilities en route to successful careers and lives.

Our mandate is to divorce ourselves from political and ideological allegiances and embrace the reality that we must create relevant schools and educational systems and structures that respond to the specific needs of students in specific communities. The liberal response to reform—which leans toward throwing more dollars at broken systems and structures that are no longer capable of being effective—completely ignores the need for serious overhaul in many areas. The moderate position—which embraces innovation but only on a test basis, for fear of moving the paradigm too quickly—is actually too tepid. The lofty conservative proposals—which are almost always underfunded and poorly implemented—must be toned down to match state and local budgets, which are expected to incorporate their fair shares in the funding of these reforms. In my view, *A Call to the Village* is one viable solution toward merging these varying perspectives into a range of possibilities for producing substantive improvements in student achievement.

MY JOURNEY

My academic, professional, and social interests are an accumulation of experiences in each sector that enable me to present a strategic guide based on cross-sectoral collaboration in school-age education. As my curricular and extracurricular interests have consistently gravitated toward strategy development and the academic needs of young people, respectively, the basis for my convictions about the role of cross-sectoral collaboration in education has formed. With a bachelor of business administration in accounting from Southern Methodist University, a master of business administration in strategic planning and finance from the Wharton School of the University of Pennsylvania, and a master of divinity from Harvard University, I have amassed a strong theoretical foundation for creating collaborative formats in varied contexts. For the past several decades, I have worked with youth in diverse organizational settings across sectors and have participated in a broad range of initiatives targeted at children in the elementary and secondary grades.

Although my own elementary and secondary years were spent in the Little Rock public school system, my work with youth for the past 15 years has spanned the metropolitan areas of Philadelphia, Boston, New York City, and Atlanta. As the chair of the Wharton School Speakers Bureau, I coordinated and participated in classroom presentations and dialogue with high school students in the west Philadelphia community for 2 years. During my tenure as a Divinity School student at Harvard, I complemented my academic interests with firsthand experiences by directing the youth programs for a local church and serving as a youth counselor for a court advocacy program in the Roxbury and Dorchester sections of Boston. As a Sunday school teacher for teenagers in Westchester County, New York, and a substitute teacher in the Atlanta suburbs, I have personally experienced the kinds of daily challenges confronted by teaching professionals. As the director of the after-school and summer programs for an independent school in metropolitan Atlanta, I have been successful at integrating these types of ancillary activities with the academic components of the regular school day.

Corporate mentoring and tutoring programs, as well as community and church initiatives that serve school-age children, provided many opportunities for me to witness the realities of everyday life as an elementary or secondary student. After spending more than a decade in corporate America and contemplating how to build a lasting and fulfilling professional career, I determined that my most sincere desire in life was to own a legacy that would allow me to make a meaningful contribution to public education. Just as academia had exposed new realities and cultures for me, I strongly believe that all youth should be given similar chances to explore and experience new ideas and choices through education. Whether through a corporate opportunity or the creation of a completely different platform, I am intent on merging my passion for young people and education with my skills in business.

My work and community-service interests have extended across the nonprofit, private, public, and religious sectors. I have worked in large multinational private firms and corporations, local churches, independent schools, and universities during my years spent in Dallas, Miami, New York, Boston, Washington, DC, and Atlanta. I have also served as a member of the loan committee for a large community development financial institution in Boston and as a financial trustee of a local church in metropolitan New York. As a certified public accountant, assistant vice president, business manager, accounting manager, and finance director, I have had ample exposure to management-level decision making by organizations in varying contexts. These broad, ranging experiences underscore my ability to understand how to effectively navigate the constraints of missions, strategies, goals, objectives, and stakeholders across organization types and sectors. My expansive professional experiences enable me to understand the priorities of each sector and to integrate these objectives into collaborative strategies that can produce tangible benefits in school-age education. With over 2 decades of professional work and academic preparation, I have witnessed the range of unique and innovative approaches being applied by people and organizations to issues such as education. These observations confirm for me the potential of cross-sectoral collaboration as a viable solution to the challenges we face in public schools.

INTRODUCTION TO CROSS-SECTORAL COLLABORATION

The motivation for developing this guide originated out of a personal desire to participate in resolving what I consider to be the most prominent public issue confronting America, which is how to make elementary and secondary schools effective once again. As I watched public education completely unravel, it became clear that what was needed was some fresh and innovative approaches to educating young people. Fortunately, many others saw it the same way—thus, the range of reform efforts being witnessed across the country. I am proposing this collaborative framework as one solution for redefining and reengineering elementary and secondary schools. I sincerely hope that many will discover that everyone has a role to play in this most critical juncture in the history of American public education. This writing is essentially a call to action to all Americans who feel a sense of ownership in making sure that all young people have equal access to high-quality education and equal opportunities to achieve academically and succeed in the constantly evolving global marketplace.

My primary objectives for this book are to (1) offer a strategic road map for individuals, institutions, and organizations that are interested in developing school prototypes as well as innovative teaching and learning models; (2) present illustrations of how organizations and professionals are already collaborating in education; (3) stimulate dialogue and the formation of partnerships across the nonprofit, private, public, and religious sectors; and (4) debunk and dispel myths that have prevented sectors from engaging one another in solving public and social problems. If this book causes parents, professionals, corporations, clergy, community activists, bureaucrats, policymakers, and social service providers to recognize the strength that lies in collaboration, then it may be deemed a successful endeavor. If these entities begin to acknowledge their interdependence, then this will signal for me the beginning of, perhaps, a broader movement toward purposeful responses to one of our more daunting challenges in this 21st century—the transformation of elementary and secondary school systems.

This practical guide is targeted at people and institutions that are seriously committed to transforming public schools. To be sure, private and public practitioners, communities of faith, policymakers, large and small companies, nonprofit organizations, entrepreneurs, and educators will, ideally, find this reading provocative because it challenges tradition, as well as concretizes many of the prevailing trends in education. My hope is that those in academia will take advantage of the interdisciplinary opportunities to enhance their teaching and learning experiences by incorporating ideas of collaboration as a viable solution to many problems being examined in the classroom. Specifically, graduate students of business, education, public policy and administration, and divinity schools and seminaries, as well as students representing many disciplines at the undergraduate level, can benefit greatly from a critical examination of collaboration. Cross-sectoral collaboration can be an effective teaching and learning methodology, especially in light of the reality that many of our social and economic dilemmas can no longer be examined through singular, isolated lenses. The globalization and cross-cultural character of today's markets and societies require multidisciplinary and global perspectives that consider relationships across disciplines and professions.

A Call to the Village is a road map for developing collaborative strategies to integrate the knowledge, ideas, expertise, resources, networks, and systems of the nonprofit, private, public, and religious sectors in the transformation of elementary and secondary schools. It is not intended as an analysis of micro (or pedagogical) topics; instead, it is a macro (or strategic) assessment of how we can successfully usher in a new paradigm of whole-school reform by engaging industries, professions, and sectors. The predominant writings related to school reform justifiably focus on micro-issues such as curricula, administration, teacher development, parental involvement, special-needs learning, standards and accountability, and school choice. Although cross-sectoral collaboration acknowledges the interconnectedness between the micro- and macro-components of school-age education, its focus is a specific niche—the building and implementation of strategic partnerships across the sectors. The increased utilization of cross-sectoral collaboration by domestic and global communities to address social, economic, and environmental challenges attests to the growing prominence of models that promote working together across sectoral boundaries.

This guide is timely because practically every entity in society is affected by the substandard academic performance of students and schools. Cross-sectoral collaboration is a viable option not only for merging nontraditional partners in the reengineering of school systems and structures but also for assisting legislatures in the financing and implementation of broad reforms. The organizational and strategic coherence of the private sector, the spiritual and moral stewardship of the religious sector, the local and social service focuses of the nonprofit sector, and the public sector's mandate to provide equitable public goods can serve as barometers for integrating the strengths of each sector to produce countless school prototypes. The faith community's ability to commit underutilized physical space for schools, the corporation's capacity to develop unique management systems, the foundation community's skill in local market funding, and the state government agency's implementation and monitoring strengths are the types of market opportunities that are untapped in public education. The potential for economies of scale, transferability of skills, and synergistic relationships is indeed vast.

Cross-sectoral collaboration is essentially a framework of strategy development and implementation, designed to build strategic partnerships for responding to the educational dilemmas of local schools and school districts. Specifically, it is a participatory approach that facilitates purposeful and coordinated educational solutions in local communities as it incorporates resources and information from entities representing multiple industries, professions, and sectors. A basic premise underlying cross-sectoral collaboration is that a collaborative approach—as opposed to a stand-alone, singular attempt—can have a dramatic impact on the effectiveness and efficiencies of education models, systems, processes, and structures. By focusing on the distinctive competencies of each institution—whether professional, sector, or industry—collaborators can draw from a broad spectrum of information, knowledge, assets, and networks, collectively represented by people and institutions.

The public will benefit from cross-sectoral collaboration because it will assist in delineating and articulating those elements of school-age education that are essential for achieving educational goals. Cross-sectoral collaboration can also be a tool for synthesizing the range of educational priorities of a community's stakeholder groups. By engaging the nonprofit, private, public, and religious sectors in the examination of education issues such as the standards, testing, and school choice debates, we allow these entities to fulfill some of their organizational and social responsibilities. Just as each sector plays an important part in the financing of public schools vis-à-vis its tax obligations, each deserves the opportunity to play a part in the redefinition of public schools across the country.

Cross-sectoral collaboration is intended to complement conventional education models that primarily incorporate the educator perspective in devising teaching and learning programs. Instead of serving as advocates or critics of the traditional education industry, professionals and organizations from other sectors should serve as participants at the front end and throughout the process of school transformation. The intent of broader sectoral participation is not to usurp or eliminate the contributions of those trained as educators but to supplement their work with that of professionals who routinely lead, manage, and work in the nonprofit, private, public, and religious sectors. This would enable the integration of ideas and perspectives of persons and organizations representing a wide spectrum of professions and industries. My proposition is that conventional wisdom and ideas about how to effectively educate and teach young people may need to be completely overhauled to keep pace with the phenomenal change that has occurred with respect to how we live, work, and play. The cultural exchanges, market globalization, information explosion, and technological revolution require an education paradigm unlike any that we have utilized to date.

The interdependence of many spheres of our lives demands that we examine school-age education utilizing a different paradigm. Implicit in cross-sectoral collaboration is the belief that the effectiveness of schools requires a seamless transition between the spheres of school and work—which is to say that we need to do a better job of integrating the academic training of our youth with the knowledge and skill requirements of the professions, industries, and sectors in which they will eventually lead, manage, and work. This framework can be a vital part of this transition because it facilitates the creation of partnerships among educators and organizations that know which skills our youth will need to be successful leaders, citizens, managers, and workers. A collaborative approach such as this would accommodate the need to incorporate fresh and innovative ideas about teaching and learning as well as enable society to develop education models that reflect the global, cultural, and social changes that have transformed our daily existence over the past several decades. One ultimate goal of this collaborative framework is to reconcile what we teach our students in the classroom with our expectations of them as they progress toward careers in the various sectors. The participation of sectors in transforming local schools is one solution for bridging the gaps between school and life beyond elementary and secondary matriculation.

❶
THE PARADIGM SHIFT IN ELEMENTARY AND SECONDARY EDUCATION

As families, educators, and communities continue to strategize about the appropriate responses to ineffective local schools, many challenges must be confronted to move beyond the fears and obstacles that have hindered us for decades. Each community's stakeholders must achieve an appropriate balance between adopting innovation versus maintaining the status quo without compromising the academic needs of the young people. All of us must demonstrate unfeigned courage in embracing innovativeness while relinquishing aspects of tradition that have stunted our children's academic growth. It is imperative that we examine the critical issues through lenses that allow us to see outside of our political ideologies and bureaucratic allegiances. Either we can choose to be proactive in setting the agenda for our young people's education, or we can engage in the usual rhetoric while the so-called educational elites continue to profit on the backs of our youth. Our children need us to stand up and be counted, by voicing their concerns and claiming their rights to an equitable and high-quality education.

As we witness the paradigmatic shift in the delivery of elementary and secondary education, it is important that we refine our education priorities in ways that acknowledge the prevailing trends and mandates of the industry. As educators have experimented with open-enrollment programs and magnet schools, the priorities surrounding school equity and equal access have been compromised because of the successes of many of these efforts. As families witness their children's poor academic performances in neighborhood schools, they become increasingly focused on selecting schools that promise strong academic achievement, without regard to the location or demographics of the schools. The expansion of school voucher initiatives and charter schools, as well as the renewed push toward increased accountability and higher standards, is occurring as parents and educators exhibit a greater inclination toward change and innovation. Unlike any point in history, school-age education requires new archetypes that integrate established academic formats with original ideas about teaching and learning. The acceptance of new school models over the past few decades is the essential precursor to the inevitable transformation in elementary and secondary education.

The clarion call has been sounded for us as a village to preserve the educational rights and potential of all children. We must continue to extend ourselves beyond traditional boundaries for our education models to address the needs of a cross-cultural, highly technical, and interdisciplinary world. Enterprises and professionals from all sectors are redefining their organizational and sectoral responsibilities to respond to the issues surrounding academic achievement, equity, access, and accountability. Beyond economic, racial, political, or bureaucratic identity, citizens are determining that the statute of limitations on certain aspects of education may be expiring. The perennial mandate for sufficiently integrated schools and equitable allocation of resources has been losing some of its momentum as alliances have developed that are based solely on the potential for high academic achievement, unlike past emphasis on conservative versus liberal values or suburban versus urban locales. Indeed, we are beholding the dawning of a new age in public education, and we must seize the opportunities to marshal and mobilize the talents and resources of all citizens, professions, industries, and sectors toward a boundless present and future for our children.

DESEGREGATION VIS-À-VIS SCHOOL EQUITY

One of the more complex and elusive aspects of the school reform debate relates to the juxtaposition of school desegregation and school equity. The desegregation mandate's goal has been to achieve equity in the distribution of educational resources, as well as equitable access to educational opportunities. After a half century of implementing and enforcing measures designed to achieve integrated and equitable classrooms, our school systems have youth who continue to be plagued by poor academic performance. One conclusion that can be drawn from this desegregation dilemma is that, perhaps, it has been successful in achieving its goal of cosmetic integration, but the task of achieving performance integration is more a function of adapting teaching and learning processes to classrooms and schools in particular communities. Some schools and school districts have been more successful or persistent than others in their focus on cosmetic integration; however, the result has, more often than not, led to minimal improvement in student academic achievement. The prevailing emphasis of school administrators and policymakers seems to be away from desegregation and balance and toward options that are designed to increase standardized-test scores. The shortfall of this strategy is that it ignores the goals of the original mandate.

Cosmetic integration can describe the extent to which we have been able to achieve equitable distribution of educational resources. Performance integration can relate to our willingness to go several steps further by creatively implementing legislative mandates as a means toward equitable outcomes across schools and school districts. Cosmetic integration—which is, effectively, de jure desegregation—has not produced balanced academic performance across the school spectrum. To realize equitable academic results, we must focus on achieving performance integration, which is essentially de facto desegregation. Our task is to examine the effects of cosmetic integration in relation to performance integration pursuant to true educational equity. We need to create a range of responses and scenarios that take into account the unique characteristics of cultures, experiences, and perspectives of students, teaching professionals, and communities.

The question may become a matter related to the systemic and structural pedagogy of the classroom and school environments, which effectively move us beyond the legal, political, and moral themes surrounding school desegregation. Our charge is not to answer whether desegregation remains an important item on the education agenda but to address whether it does so at the expense of ensuring a teaching and learning environment that is conducive to high academic performance. We must be astute enough to discern when we are being cajoled or bamboozled into compromising our most important priorities. It is no longer sufficient for us to support desegregation solely for the sake of achieving integrated classrooms, especially in light of the fact that integrated classrooms have not resulted in high academic performance from our students across racial and economic groups.

Despite our progress toward fulfilling the original mandate, the preeminent question remains: Does desegregation presuppose school equity? In my view, the answer to this question is a resounding *No!* Indeed, many other factors may account for the inequities across schools (e.g., differences in tax bases and state funding, differences in teacher requirements across states); but where states have taken steps to compensate for funding inequities and equalize teacher requirements, there are still substantial gaps in student academic performance. For several decades beyond the desegregation mandate, elementary and secondary education was considered to be effective, to the point where we witnessed strong student achievement across a broad spectrum of demographic groups and felt pretty good about the efficacy of our educational systems. Although not all students were experiencing high levels of success, proportionately, strong academic performances were seen in virtually every economic or social subgroup. Without regard to the nature of the cause for the demise, it remains primarily the responsibility of our educators to develop meaningful responses that will transform how our teachers teach and how our children learn.

We have enough experiences to know that the desegregation edict has not been and can never be a panacea for academic equity. The goals of resource and outcome equity continue to be the most formidable challenges confronting us in public education. Our task is to move beyond the rhetoric toward a focus on why our young people remain academic underperformers in an era that is characterized by unprecedented per-pupil expenditures in many regions of the nation. Our immediate task is to expand how we complete desegregation by allowing freedom of choice and the creation of innovative nontraditional schools. We must determine whether we are willing to accept a broader interpretation of desegregation to include school prototypes that have unique missions and programs designed to meet the diverse needs of all children. We must be open to new approaches for sharing, and we must exchange across schools and school districts as a means toward de facto desegregation.

The salient question does not pertain solely to achieving equitable resource allocation, because the achievement of equitable academic outcomes is, essentially, the more appropriate concern. The reality is that most states are taking steps to ensure equitable resources for all schools, so we cannot remain fixated on this point. We must be open to the best possible solutions for our schools regardless of the cosmetic effects imposed on the student population. Ideally, we prefer schools that are adequately integrated, but the reality is that we have an unintended mandate to move beyond a desegregation emphasis and toward a focus on achieving high academic performance in all schools. Our constantly changing world and the advanced levels of knowledge and skills required to succeed make it imperative that we expand our approach beyond cosmetics. Cross-sectoral collaboration can assist in the achievement of equitable resource allocation, as well as equitable academic outcomes. Collaboration and interaction across schools and school systems can ensure that students from varying demographic groups gain access to academic resources and experiences that may not have been otherwise available to them. Intra- and interdistrict partnerships are one solution to the prevailing inequities that result in the achievement disparities that plague some groups of students.

ACCOUNTABILITY, STANDARDS, AND TESTING

The debate pertaining to the implementation of improved accountability systems and the application of higher academic standards and testing has evolved into a movement of its own. The momentum of these discussions has become so pronounced that the focus is no longer being placed on what is actually broken in schools. Until stakeholders are willing to eliminate the inadequacies in the classrooms and schools, there can be no significant improvement in student achievement. Any attempt to apply new standards without resolving extant systemic and structural deficiencies is absolutely faulty and ludicrous. Although it is true that many teaching professionals apply low standards to their students and many administrators have not held the classroom teachers accountable to high enough standards, these are not the sole reasons for students' substandard academic performance. The ineffective structures, systems, and processes of public schools bear significant responsibility for the low levels of achievement. Cross-sectoral collaboration can help alleviate some of the classroom and school deficiencies by encouraging the participation of (1) professionals who are proficient in those areas where schools are weak and (2) sectors that utilize systems that are transferable to school operations.

How can we realistically expect students to succeed in classrooms while they sit in wobbly chairs, read books with torn pages, and attend schools with leaking ceilings? These illustrations are the reality for many school-age children across America. The real tragedy, though, is that legislators and others know that these conditions exist, but they nevertheless proceed with the imposition of stricter standards and more testing. In the name of equity, justice, and fairness, no school or its students should be evaluated when the teaching and learning conditions have been compromised and the school culture is neither safe nor comfortable. Our goals for improving student, teacher, and school performance ought to include a desire to make the process operate more efficiently and effectively. Our vested interests in the movement toward increased standards and assessments ought not to be politically motivated but should ideally reflect a sincere concern for and commitment to the education of our youth. By building partnerships among persons and organizations that represent multiple professions, industries, and sectors, we can collectively address the multitude of weaknesses throughout our educational systems and structures.

The acknowledgment of inadequacies in the hardware and software components of elementary and secondary education creates a reasonable starting point for seriously responding to the need for true school accountability, higher academic standards, and meaningful assessment tools. Components such as teacher recruitment, classroom reengineering, and facilities renovation represent root problems that must be corrected before applying any form of increased standards. An initial focus on the symptoms of failing schools without paying adequate attention to the causes of low-performing schools is a meaningless endeavor at the outset. Such an outside-in approach can provide only a Band-Aid remedy to the multidimensional problems in our schools. This basically places the cart (i.e., academic achievement, standards and assessments) before the horse (i.e., school hardware and software). Conversely, an inside-out approach can identify and correct those elements in the process that are not functioning well, thereby resulting in a meaningful assessment of student and teacher performance in the context of sufficient tools and resources.

Without question, the systems of accountability and performance standards being applied to our students, schools, and teaching professionals must be elevated if we expect our youth to be able to lead and perform in a world that has evolved into an interdisciplinary, cross-cultural, and technologically advanced global marketplace. Every aspect of the process has to be enhanced to ensure that the necessary resources are accessible to accommodate the increased expectations. Although there may be many alternatives for achieving the desired outcomes, the implementation of higher standards and tighter accountability systems, in conjunction with comprehensive systemic reform, is a necessity for elevating our public schools. Those who support higher standards and stricter accountability without addressing the systemic and structural deficiencies in schools do not appear to be interested in comprehensive reform. Similarly, those who oppose raising standards and increased accountability without offering any alternative approaches do nothing but harbor low expectations of the students. Whatever road maps we choose, we must do our best to ensure the successful nurturing of the intellectual, academic, athletic, and artistic abilities of all school-age children.

GLOBAL AND LIFESTYLE CHANGES

The globalization of markets and the growing prominence of information and technology in our lives require a departure from our customary ways of educating youth. The competitiveness throughout the international marketplace is demanding a highly skilled, informed, and trained workforce that can readily adjust to cultural and demographic differences. As markets and cultures increasingly exchange ideas and share products, our need to interpret diverse interests and attributes becomes a key concern in global communication and trade. The intellectual, technical, and professional demands that are accompanying many of these changes demonstrate how high the bar has been set for minimum skill levels. Elementary, secondary, and postsecondary education must create effective ways of preparing students to succeed in professions that require highly skilled workers. Educators cannot afford to sit around and hypothesize about school reform as external markets and cultures continue to expand rapidly. Our schools and school systems must adapt to the change in order to properly train young people to lead and manage in a constantly evolving global landscape.

From industrialization to the extant technological revolution, we have witnessed a phenomenal elevation of knowledge and skill requirements throughout the industries and professions. The complexities and interdependence that characterize so many markets and sectors have basically transformed how organizations conduct routine operations. Globalization, immigration, and transcontinental trade have enhanced our cross-cultural learning and have enabled us to enjoy new economies and synergies that were nonexistent in decades past. The vertical and horizontal integration of multinational corporations make it possible for a single entity's products to be produced, distributed, and sold on different continents. The global transference of information, technology, and culture has essentially created a proliferation of knowledge, ideas, products, services, and experiences that transcend geographic boundaries. This information and cultural explosion is producing infinite possibilities for groups and individuals on all levels. More important, the prevailing global trends establish a practical foundation from which firms and individuals can build collaborative relationships for the benefit of improving public education. The convergence of markets has forced organizations to form relationships beyond their usual boundaries.

Our transition from a slower-paced and compartmentalized society of past years to the existing highly technical, fast-paced, and integrated culture warrants new approaches to elementary and secondary education that incorporate the effects of these lifestyle changes. The prevalence of technology is, perhaps, the more prominent aspect of our shift toward becoming a society that processes information and transactions at incredible speeds. Although this quicker pace affects how firms and individuals make decisions, it underscores how important it is for us to adjust our education processes to reflect the kind of world that students can anticipate beyond academia. The conventional methods of teaching that have not historically accounted for differences in learning styles and learning paces must be revised to allow for customized instructional programs for students with diverse aptitudes and abilities. Through the application of technology and information-based systems, the specific learning needs of students can be matched with modes of instruction that are based on a child's documented developmental process. Electronically based methods of instruction, evaluation, and reporting can accommodate teachers and administrators' needs to examine vast amounts of student data. In the absence of the information and technology revolution, educators could never manage the volume of data that they are being forced to process in the existing climate.

SECTORAL CHANGES

The increasing interdependence across markets and sectors represents enormous opportunities for collaboration among nonprofit-, private-, public-, and religious-sector entities and professionals. As we began the new century, we discovered that, not only were public-sector educators and organizations concerned about the low academic performance of students, but many professionals and companies from other sectors were troubled as well and were in fact taking meaningful steps to demonstrate their commitment to reform. A sizable number of private companies are managing schools, school districts, or certain aspects of school operations across many states. Although many school officials and communities have been somewhat reluctant about private-sector participation in public school management, the results to date have shown some promise for these ventures. The consolidations that have taken place among school management companies can be viewed as an indication that these firms intend to be permanent players in public education. Their willingness to partner with seasoned educators in the development of comprehensive reform models should lead to substantive improvements in student achievement.

Communities of faith and nonprofit organizations are opening schools as a way of responding to the need to build sustainable institutions in neighborhoods and communities. The inability of local schools to provide youth with basic academic training has motivated community institutions to develop schools themselves, instead of relying on school officials who have not exhibited a propensity toward considerable school reform. Local churches and nonprofits are realizing that the longer it takes school systems to make the necessary changes, the further behind students get, which stunts their academic development and, ultimately, the productivity of the larger community. Entrepreneurs are demonstrating their commitment to raising academic achievement by funding voucher and scholarship programs that subsidize student enrollment in private, independent, and parochial schools. The objective of these programs is to move students out of nonperforming public schools and into academic settings that provide them with the tools to excel academically. The success and further adoption of voucher and scholarship initiatives depend largely on whether student achievement improves as a result of enrollment in these new schools.

Perhaps, the most encouraging phenomenon surrounding the changing landscape is that participating entities are moving beyond the rhetoric and toward the creation of school models that are relevant to the academic needs of students in their respective areas. Given that citizens have expressed dissatisfaction with the state of public schools for a long time, recent trends seem to indicate that they have finally realized that many in the education industry do not intend to implement the kinds of comprehensive reforms that will lead to successful schooling. For many, the hope is that they can force the education industry to change by proving the success of innovative ideas and programs through external models. In some cases, organizations are tapping into public school funding by applying for a charter, whereas others are investing large portions of their personal fortunes to introduce original models. These diverse education proposals not only reflect a broad consensus concerning the need for large-scale school reform but also demonstrate the varied ways in which sectors interpret their social responsibility to public education.

Private-sector participation in education has traditionally focused on opening an on-site school, adopting a local school, supplying professional mentors, or developing after-school programs. Corporations customarily invest time and money into philanthropic activities that emphasize the academic achievement of school-age children. The heightened global competitiveness and technological revolution have shifted the playing field in ways that require companies to be more proactive about education issues and concerns. As firms acknowledge the changing dynamics of global markets, they are taking major steps to voice their concerns about failing public schools and how such schools should be reformed. A new trend among private companies is their growing involvement in efforts that directly affect the academic preparation of their future workers and managers. Executives are collaborating with graduate schools, school superintendents, policymakers, and leaders in other industries to develop strategic formulas for addressing the weaknesses in local schools. Private-sector enterprises know that to maintain their global preeminence, they must continue to hire intellectually and technically strong workers and managers. If we do not elevate the state of elementary and secondary schools, the future workers in private industry will not possess the fundamental skills and abilities necessary for management and leadership.

The nonprofit sector is experiencing unprecedented visibility and viability as a result of its capacity to (1) close economic gaps that occur as a result of market inefficiencies and (2) fill voids created by inadequacies of public programs. The sector's ability to provide products and services that are typically within the domain of private-sector or public-sector enterprises underscores the indispensability of nonprofits. The proximity of local nonprofits to neighborhoods and communities gives them a tremendous advantage in terms of understanding the specific needs of constituent groups within communities. The local expertise of community development enterprises is allowing them to provide housing, income, and investment products for clients who are routinely underserved by other sectors. Social service providers are able to streamline their services in ways that respond to unique attributes of local residents. An important development occurring throughout the sector is the expansion of organizational missions to encompass funding of education-related initiatives. Foundations have historically been strong supporters of K–12 programs; however, community development financial institutions are just beginning to review more education proposals for funding.

As churches and other faith communities move beyond their walls and outside of their traditional boxes, they are creating their own schools in larger numbers; partnering with other entities to produce new prototypes;

and developing ancillary educational programs to address tutoring, mentoring, artistic, athletic, after-school, and various other specialized academic and extracurricular programs. Churches are also discovering that to remain relevant in people's lives and to nurture the whole person, their ministerial mandates must encompass the social and economic needs of their parishioners. The growth of church nonprofit subsidiaries as community or economic development corporations is providing religious organizations with a channel for participating in social and economic ventures that should not be merged with religious activities. By establishing these subsidiaries, churches have been able to access public and private funding that allows them to offer services such as affordable housing, banking, small-business consulting, and employment services. As the religious community takes a proactive stance around issues affecting its constituents, it finds nonprofit, private, and public partners willing to collaborate in projects that provide a range of community products and services. Churches are collaborating with community organizations to create neighborhood schools that will prepare the youth of their communities to excel academically.

The public sector's traditional role of being the chief provider of elementary and secondary education has not changed but is being complemented by the work of persons and organizations from other sectors. The introduction of diverse school options in communities across the nation reflects the willingness by so many to engage in all sorts of ventures that are targeted at school reform. Administrators and teaching professionals are working with partners who can provide critical leadership and innovative ideas about areas that are ineffective. In many instances, we are already witnessing the collaboration of school management companies and schools to revise components of school processes that affect student academic achievement. Classroom sizes are being adjusted to allow for greater student–teacher interaction and more focused instruction. Curriculum packages in reading and mathematics that have high success rates are being adopted. Education administrators at the federal level are working closely with state and local education officials to implement federally mandated standards pertaining to student achievement levels. Whether intended or not, public-sector education officials at all levels are collaborating in good faith to ensure that federal mandates are at least given a fair chance to succeed.

The growth of public–private partnerships, the increased visibility of the nonprofit community, and the emergence of the religious community beyond its walls underscore the potential of cross-sectoral partnerships as effective vehicles for resolving inefficiencies and ineffectiveness in education. The private sector's emphasis on organizational and strategic coherence, the religious sector's commitment to spiritual and moral stewardship, the nonprofit sector's local and social service focuses, and the public sector's charge to provide equitable public goods can be successfully integrated to produce countless approaches to enhancing school systems, processes, programs, and structures. Each sector's unique strengths and resources, coupled with its interest in yielding high-quality public schools, can create measurable value and produce synergies with other sectors that enable a range of strategic options that transcend sectoral boundaries. The nonprofit community's capacity to supplement the work of the private sector and public sector points to the potential of collaboration across sectors. Likewise, the religious community's efforts to engage private-sector partners in multidimensional ventures highlight its willingness to move beyond tradition to fulfill its ministerial mandates. The convergence of sectors around community building has laid a foundation on which we can build effective collaboration across sectors pursuant to transforming elementary and secondary schools. Collaborative frameworks can serve as forums for interpreting the growing complexities and educational options that confront families, communities, and educators.

2

STRATEGIC ALTERNATIVES: MARKET- VERSUS SYSTEM-BASED REFORM

The elementary and secondary education paradigm of the 20th century is no longer applicable. Although it may not be necessary to wholly dismantle extant educational structures and systems, it does make sense to reconfigure the existing infrastructure in ways that can lead to formats that are useful for teaching and learning in the 21st century. By integrating the best of system- and market-based reforms into our schools, we can produce models that accommodate the needs of young people in our urban, suburban, and rural communities nationwide. The combination of systemic and market reforms should move us closer to a public education landscape that ensures equity and access for every student. Both approaches must continue to be employed concurrently to create avenues of change within and without our school districts. Market, or choice, reforms are needed to force us to examine nontraditional means of school enhancement, whereas systemic reforms are needed to implement necessary changes within existing school structures. Market-based initiatives provide us with greater freedom and choice beyond traditional public schools, whereas systemic improvements complement the choices already available to us. Where public schools do not respond to new systems, standards, and structures, market choices must be available to families as a means of filling the void that is the result of systemic weaknesses in schools. Similarly, choice models that neither improve academic results nor meet standards comparable to those being applied to existing schools must be eliminated. The execution of both market and systemic reforms is fundamentally a checks-and-balances process that enables the testing of school prototypes while employing innovative systems within the existing infrastructure. The influx of fresh ideas from practitioners and various other noneducation organizations makes the education marketplace much more competitive and should translate into improved schools and higher academic performance from students, on a large scale. The application of relevant systemic reforms and the inclusion of viable choice alternatives can lead to an education landscape that responds to the diverse needs of many students while also moving us closer to understanding and resolving our public education quagmire.

MARKET-BASED ALTERNATIVES

The market-based approach to school reform is designed to inject competition into public education by providing students, parents, and teachers with an array of school choices. Additionally, market responses allow us to incorporate systems and structures from the private sector that are intended to produce greater effectiveness and efficiencies. For those of us who are committed to building effective public schools, we must assess the extent to which we believe such market competition can enhance public education. Specifically, we need to evaluate whether our goals are consistent with those of the persons and organizations that are presenting the choices. We must acknowledge that a private company's capacity to produce private goods does not preclude it from being an effective deliverer of a public good such as education. Conversely, because a company has been successful in the private sector does not guarantee success in developing and managing public schools. Clearly, individual circumstances and community dynamics will dictate different models for different communities.

As market-oriented reform models become prevalent, we must be persistent about maintaining the integrity of elementary and secondary education by not allowing private interests to supersede the academic needs of our youth. As more entrepreneurs and private companies seek to manage or create school prototypes, they will need to ascertain and adhere to the dimensions of education that set public goods apart from private goods. For example, we must ensure that the principles of equity and fairness, as well as the emphases on high academic expectations and performance, are paramount in any venture. Educators and communities have a responsibility to reinforce the importance of these aspects of education. Although many private companies and entrepreneurs may easily detect the range of systemic opportunities in elementary and secondary school operations, it is incumbent on those who have significant experience in education to begin to dialogue with and inform newcomers as to how school operations differ from other organizational forms. For example, the demographics of urban, suburban, and rural schools vary in ways that dictate hiring faculty who possess specialized training, thus driving up faculty salaries and lowering the profit potential for a private company seeking a return on its investment. Similarly, the prevailing emphasis on smaller classroom sizes would have a negative effect on the bottom line of a private company because this approach requires more faculty hiring to maintain a targeted teacher–pupil ratio. These are some examples of the unique features of public education that require a focus on goals and objectives of teaching and learning regardless of the incremental costs. Most private companies reconcile incurring additional costs in terms of the incremental profits attached to them; this type of reconciliation does not always take place in school administration. Ensuring the integrity of school-age education by maintaining its unique characteristics must be a priority and must not be relegated to a lesser role because of ancillary motives such as return on investment.

Traditional schools can benefit greatly by utilizing various management and operational systems currently employed in private markets, so long as these processes and techniques are implemented in ways that complement the uniqueness of education. Formats that can be applicable to school settings include compensation and incentive models, input and output measurement tools, resource utilization processes, distribution systems, technology and software applications, and cost-sharing approaches. Public schools can learn a lot from the medical community in terms of how to budget or finance costly components of its operations. Hospitals have been able to offer highly specialized and technologically advanced medical procedures to their clientele because of a willingness to create ways of cost sharing across neighboring medical facilities. Similar to those of schools, the budgetary constraints do not allow for the purchase of expensive medical equipment. Many schools and school districts might be in a better position to incorporate technology if they examined ways of sharing or spreading the costs across schools and communities. Likewise, specialized faculty and staff may be more affordable if considered in the context of shared costs across a number of schools—for example, special-needs instructors, social service and medical providers, and instrumental-music and dramatic-arts professionals.

One must be certain that educating students is the primary objective over and above profit maximization for individuals and companies. Although many have criticized market approaches solely on the basis of the providers' intention to make a profit, such a singular focus has distorted the real debate, which is whether these providers can actually produce high academic achievement from our students. To be sure, the very essence of private enterprise is to manage its resources in a manner that leads to profitability. There is a market segmentation occurring in education whereby models such as open enrollment and magnet schools are being supplemented by scores of charter schools and voucher programs. Families are being introduced to a multitude of choices that not only emulate the traditional classroom setting but reinvent teaching and learning processes altogether.

The defining characteristic of our children's successes has more to do with whether a school is conducive to high academic achievement and less to do with whether a school is public, private, independent, or parochial. To the extent that school models address clearly definable needs, market-based reforms that allow freedom of choice and promise access to high-quality education will continue to garner widespread public acceptance. We can no longer allow ourselves to be shackled by tradition and coerced by self-interests that attempt to dictate who should be allowed to manage and reform our schools. We must be willing to engage new partners and new approaches to resolve dilemmas that are decades old. The statute of limitations has expired on school districts, governmental bodies, and the educational elites. Our young people deserve schools that will prepare them for leadership, professional life, and productive citizenship.

Charter Schools

The debate regarding whether the expansion of school choice is a threat to public education highlights the complexity surrounding many of the new options. Families and teachers are opting for the charter school environment because it promises them improved academic results, accountability, freedom, and flexibility. Although the quality of charters varies significantly, there are some impressive and comprehensive models in the marketplace. Although charters are fundamentally innovative public schools, many representing the educational establishment view them as anathema to the status quo. One major point of contention is the reality that charter schools operate outside of local district regulations and bureaucracies and are often accountable to an independent state-appointed entity that approves and renews charter applications and monitors the operations and finances of the schools. Additionally, the belief that charter schools drain dollars from existing public schools is a prominent concern of opponents.

The intended goal of charters is to implement new approaches to teaching and learning in a public school setting, using the same per-pupil expenditures as traditional public schools. Furthermore, where charter schools improve academic performance or meet their stated goals and objectives, school districts are expected to replicate the successful models in nonchartered schools throughout a district. Administrators have essentially concluded that innovativeness, as opposed to reinventing traditional approaches, is worthy of being tested. By authorizing a limited number of charters, school officials and legislators control the degree of exposure and the amount of money allocated to these experiments. Many critics have placed unreasonable timetables on the performance of charters, expecting to see academic improvements in 1 to 3 years. Not only is such a short time frame impossible, but it assumes immediate start-up and implementation phases. I argue that 5 years of operations is a more reasonable amount of time to evaluate the effectiveness of any start-up in any industry. Whereas school and local officials are inclined to allow less time, a charter has virtually no chance for success.

Charter schools do continue the use of public dollars for public schools; however, because many of the persons and organizations being awarded charters are private entrepreneurs or enterprises, some argue that this shifts taxpayer dollars into the hands of the private sector. The appropriate question is not whether private entities should be allowed to manage public schools but whether these entities can produce schools that will improve academic performance. The irony surrounding the complaint that dollars are being shifted into the hands of the private sector is that the public sector (i.e., the government) routinely shifts taxpayer dollars into the hands of private individuals and companies. Our government recognizes the utility, whether legitimate or not, inherent in many practices and processes being employed across private industry. The state or local body that is charged with overseeing charters can implement means of monitoring to assess misuse or misappropriation of public funds by charter schools. At the end of the day, the critical concern ought to be how well a charter performs in terms of the academic progress of a student body. Because we currently do not have the luxury of pointing to public school models that are consistently performing well across demographic groups, we must allow space for innovation and change. The reality is that many communities, administrators, and parents do not know which way to turn. Charter operators are simply offering one more option among many in the market.

The KIPP (Knowledge Is Power Program) academies are some of the more visible and innovative charter schools in the country. Through their utilization of consistently applied core operating principles, KIPP schools and students are being recognized for their records of high student achievement and above-average college matriculation rates. The emphasis on a safe and structured learning environment, increased time in school, and high-quality teachers has contributed to the academic gains of KIPP academies. By locating the schools in markets where students have been underserved, this network of innovative public schools is establishing a workable model for improving the academic performance of youth in public school markets that have been traditionally neglected.

Voucher Programs

For some critics of school reform, charter schools and voucher programs are different shades of the same color because both formats are viewed as attempts to use taxpayer dollars to benefit private or religious interests. Charters are not intended to misappropriate public dollars but designed to utilize taxpayer dollars more efficiently and effectively by allowing private companies and individuals to develop new school models. Conversely, voucher programs do transfer public school dollars to private, independent, and parochial schools and are intended to affect public schools indirectly. The widely held belief is that by providing students and parents with a voucher to attend a nonpublic school, public schools will be forced to improve. To the extent that these programs can cause failing school systems to reform, they are appealing. Moreover, where they provide families with an alternative to ineffective schools, vouchers possess merit. Given that many nonpublic schools offer broad and challenging academic programs that lead to high levels of academic success, vouchers indeed play a key role in providing our children with access to meaningful educational experiences. For school districts that have not demonstrated the propensity to implement substantive reform measures, school vouchers represent greater access to better schools and more freedom of choice for families. Although these programs do not make provisions for an entire student population, they do provide some relief for a targeted number of students. As we examine the full range of choices stemming from voucher initiatives, we must caution ourselves against privileging certain school types over others. Whether we choose a public, private, independent, or parochial school should depend more on the unique features of the school and less on the school classification.

The cultural, economic, and social dimensions related to school-age education and their implications have not been given sufficient attention and resources in the voucher movement. Indeed, attending a nonpublic school is quite often a different experience from that of attending a public school. Any astute observer of education knows that one cannot merely place a child who is an average student in certain school environments and expect that child to immediately become an above-average academic performer, especially given the emotional and psychological effects that environmental change has on school-age children. It is worth noting that there are always exceptional children who can rise above any circumstance. In addition to the reality that students who are attending nonpublic schools are more likely to be at least average academic performers, private, independent, and parochial school families tend to be middle- to upper-income earners. The academic culture of these schools, coupled with the economic status of many of the families, is a definite factor that should always be considered when integrating students who may be accustomed to less-than-challenging academic curricula and whose families may be in the working-poor or lower-class economic strata. Furthermore, the need to feel a sense of belonging and to develop friendships carries its own social pressures for young people. Although the emotional, psychological, cultural, economic, and social realities can be either intimidating or emboldening, a school-age child's response to these realities can be largely influential in how effective any voucher program is deemed to be.

Vouchers do not provide funding for the full range of academic and nonacademic costs associated with attending a nonpublic school. Although public schools provide busing services to and from school, parents are mostly required to provide their own means of transportation in the case of private, independent, and parochial school enrollment. For many families, this requirement is logistically or financially infeasible. The transition from a public school environment not marked by high expectations nor challenging academics to a private school setting marked by academic rigor can be a culture shock for many students. The need for academic support staff such as tutors or mentors is not often accounted for in voucher initiatives. The range of extracurricular fees can also be intimidating for a family that has limited income and minimal financial assistance. Because many private schools charge separate fees for specialized instruction (e.g., foreign languages, instrumental music, test preparation, advanced courses), students with the vouchers may have to opt out of these specialized services, thus perpetuating the gap between the haves and have-nots. Unless there is an incentive for private schools to waive the additional enrollment and attendance costs, voucher recipients will never be in a position to compete on a level playing field, especially given that the majority of their parents cannot afford the additional transportation, academic, and extracurricular expenses.

The entrepreneurs and organizations that are funding existing voucher programs believe that they can make a difference in elementary and secondary education, either by causing low-performing schools to follow their lead or by providing a means to higher academic achievement for a targeted number of students. Although their voucher programs will assist in exposing a select number of students to a new academic environment, these programs are absolutely less than optimal for the various reasons already described. If a family has to choose between remaining at a low-performing school and accepting a voucher to a private school, then, more likely than not, that family will choose the private school and attempt to make personal and financial adjustments along the way. Ultimately, if the voucher movement does nothing but cause public school administrators to examine their failures and reinvent teaching and learning processes, then voucher proponents will have done what they set out to do and will have contributed to the improvement of public elementary and secondary schools.

SYSTEM-BASED ALTERNATIVES

Similar to market-based alternatives in the industry, system-based approaches are designed to challenge the traditional public school framework by introducing systems and structures that can be effective at enhancing teaching and learning. Systemic reforms implement new processes and techniques into existing schools, whereas market reforms provide additional school choices via access to nonpublic schools and innovative public school prototypes. To achieve preeminence in public education, our task continues to be the development of more effective systems of teacher recruiting and training, while implementing systems that reward and promote teachers in a manner consistent with the academic success of students. We must also continue to establish standards, evaluation methods, and accountability systems that propel students and teachers to higher performance levels, while providing them with the tools and resources to get them there. It would be absolute folly for us to impose higher standards on teachers and students and not raise the standards of the classrooms and buildings in which they teach and learn. Systemic reforms will not work in the absence of a curriculum that is designed to give every student a fair chance at academic success, nor will it work if we fail to ensure a school culture marked by discipline, safety, and security.

The systemic reform debate must be expanded beyond the implementation of higher standards, better assessments, and public accountability systems to move toward correcting more than the mere symptoms (e.g., low academic achievement) of inadequate schools. To examine and correct the causes of low-performing schools, we must inject the reality that existing curricula need to be enhanced, school facilities require renovations and upgrades, and classrooms need to be reengineered before anyone can expect improved academic performance. School systems are indeed broken (often shattered) in many areas, and the imposition of higher standards alone is not going to fix them. It is unfair for the public to support enhanced student evaluations and accountability without supporting the provision of adequate tools and resources to accommodate these improved methods of assessment. Such an outside-in approach to systemic reform does indeed put the cart before the horse and hints at an authoritarian posture that is doomed at the outset. Conversely, what is needed is an inside-out approach that conveys a sense of compassion and willingness to work collaboratively and comprehensively in determining which elements of the overall educational system are broken. Students and teachers deserve the chance to excel in environments that are conducive to high levels of academic success and unimpeded by lack of resources and systemic neglect.

Teaching Professionals

Training and development. The classroom teacher is largely the driving force behind how well classroom activities are integrated into an overall learning plan. A teaching professional's capacity to develop lessons and activities that produce meaningful learning opportunities for students is a key determinant in whether any learning actually takes place. Students' interest in sharing and interacting with their classmates is largely a derivative of how well an instructor is able to create and innovate. This does not in any way implicate classroom teachers for the many challenges in the classroom; however, these realities do serve as a reminder that teachers play a critical role in the academic performance of young people. Policymakers, schools of education, and administrators must partner with teachers and provide strong leadership for teaching professionals to fulfill their mandates; this includes ensuring that teachers have access to sufficient tools, skills, and resources. As managers of the classroom, teachers are primarily responsible for devising appropriate classroom layouts, teaching styles, student evaluation methods, and curricula. Creating and managing these different components while serving as stewards over a group of K–12 students cannot be an enviable task. Their ability or inability to be effective in the classroom can be energizing and fulfilling for them and students alike, or it can cause the instructors to become complacent and apathetic, which eventually causes students to suffer academically. Mitigating the anxiety and frustration being experienced by so many in our teacher corps is consistently a major concern throughout the education industry.

Schools of education and other teacher development entities are continuing to reexamine and reinvent how they train classroom instructors. Training and development programs are expanding to include topics such as technology applications in education, school administration, and operations management. The move toward more comprehensive approaches to teacher professional development is creating a better understanding of and appreciation for the impact of nonacademic issues on the overall training of students in a globally integrated and technologically advanced world. Many training and development reevaluations incorporate the expertise of professionals outside of the education industry because these persons possess invaluable insight into what is needed from students to be productive in various types of professions and organizations. Also, many of these professionals are trained in areas that can assist teachers in managing the social, emotional, and psychological factors affecting young people's lives. Separately, by collaborating with graduate programs across college and university campuses, schools of education have been able to integrate new ideas and realities that extend across academic disciplines. Enhancements in teacher training are not intended to imply that more years in the academy would be a panacea for producing highly qualified professionals. Instead, many of the new approaches aim to integrate more practical components into professional development, such as the utilization of clerkships, fieldwork, and internships.

As we move toward redefining teaching as a viable profession, we should strive to institute and maintain a level of ethics, integrity, and standards that will justify the professionalization of a vocation that has been marginalized for far too long. Raising the bar for teaching professionals does not require the implementation of numerous licenses and certifications; however, it should demand uniformity in licensure and certification requirements, to communicate to the public that a systematic module for teacher development and evaluation is the goal. Consistent with this move toward professionalization is the need to raise the standard for compensation. The salary levels for classroom instructors should mirror the market value that we attach to the profession as a whole. For example, because we hold our medical and legal professionals in such high esteem, we compensate them handsomely for their services. For some inexplicable reason, our society has consistently acknowledged the extreme importance of teachers in our lives, but it has failed to elevate their salaries in a way that communicates how valuable their services are. There has to be a serious labor market correction for teacher salaries and other related forms of incentive compensation if we are indeed serious about elevating the teaching profession.

Ensuring that our teachers possess the requisite skills and have ready access to the tools and resources needed to fulfill their professional responsibilities must be our primary focus. We cannot be misguided or distracted by some who proclaim that merely raising the standards and increasing accountability will solve our problems. Our schools' records of low achievement have not been solely (nor primarily) the result of low standards and no accountability. My proposition is that the education industry (i.e., administrators, policymakers, schools of education, teacher organizations) has done a poor job of preparing and supporting teachers so that they can be successful in the classroom. When we engage in a comprehensive restructuring of our teacher training and development programs, we will move closer to fulfilling our responsibilities to classroom teachers.

A large part of the restructuring has to center on the recognition that teachers are confronted on a daily basis with varied and diverse sets of experiences and circumstances through their students. Although many educators have always believed in the one-size-fits-all theory regarding a classroom setting, this presumption has never been and continues not to be realistic. The range of cultures and contexts that accompany young people to school every day beckons for professionals who are adequately trained to discern and detect what is appropriate for different groups of students. Academic and nonacademic professional development that takes into account the need to develop instructor attributes such as creativity, adaptability, openness, and fairness will assist the professionals as they seek to expose and nurture the gifts, talents, and abilities of their students. Indeed, training that incorporates experiential modules, exposure to the economic and ethnic diversity of children, and the intellectual and sociological dimensions of K–12 education should figure prominently in contemporary teacher development programs. Also, emphasis on the interrelatedness of academic and professional disciplines is imperative as we maintain and affirm the relevance of K–12 education.

A separate focal point for teacher training programs ought to be around the issues and themes implicit in a global economy and multicultural existence. Our instructors need to be educated about the relationships across economies, cultures, and professions. Their understanding of these relationships can produce a student body that is more prepared to function globally and in a multicultural world. Raising the bar for training will result in a more comprehensive academic program that not only mandates preparation in a specific academic subject but also requires one to interpret the interdisciplinary and cross-cultural realities of a cosmopolitan world. Furthermore, interpreting and translating the economic, social, and political dimensions of topics being covered in school-age education is a skill that each teacher must hone going forward. This will essentially raise the level of discourse in our classrooms and simultaneously elevate the academic expectations and performances of students.

Preparing teaching professionals to be sensitive to and aware of difference and diversity is another dimension of training that must be emphasized in a multicultural and multiethnic world. The challenge for many is how to divorce oneself, momentarily, from one's own jaded beliefs and opinions to provide students with the most objective learning experiences possible. There always exists a subconscious tendency to bring one's learned biases and stereotypes into the education process, intentional or not. This inclination can conceivably undermine one's ability to manage the classroom in a way that is fair and accessible for every student. Teachers' preconceived and learned misconceptions about groups of students can lead to low expectations of the students, inadequate curriculum exposure, unfair evaluation methods, and nonreciprocal teacher–student discourse. Teachers' low expectations of some students and not others must be challenged and dispelled so that every student can be given a fair and equal opportunity to be academically successful. Determining how to manage the classroom in a way that is fair and that provides optimal learning opportunities for every child can be accomplished where there is a sensitivity to and respect for experiences and perspectives that are unlike one's own. When our teaching professionals are able to silence their own biases, they place themselves in a better position to hear and discern the windows of learning that exist for every child.

Teachers' beliefs, prejudices, and life experiences inform their views of students and the character of the classroom activities being employed. The environments in which many of our teachers live versus those of their students can often be separated by several degrees. This reality signals one of the primary dilemmas in education, which is how to bridge the gap between the everyday realities of teacher and student and the need to devise effective teaching and learning methodologies within these contexts. A classroom teacher's inability to comprehend and interpret the nuances and themes that compose the contemporary youth world can produce a degree of irrelevance and ineffectiveness in the classroom—which is to say, when one does not devise learning approaches that utilize some of the language, customs, mores, and so on, that are recognizable to students, then the likelihood of being able to make an initial connection with students can be limited. It is absolutely true that students need to be able to learn outside of the norms and traditions to which they have grown accustomed; however, the reality confronting educators today is that young people are quite distracted and we need to devise means of getting their attention back. Many of the students who are underperforming are marching to very different drumbeats, and it is the educator's responsibility to make a workable connection with them.

We desperately need to challenge and elevate the intellectual exercises of school-age children in a way that causes them to begin to think critically at an earlier age so that as they progress, they are in a position to build on what has been previously exposed and analyzed. This must be done in a manner that does not compromise the existing intellectual abilities of the students but does tap into their latent and underutilized intellectual curiosity. Indeed, learning is very much one's ability and willingness to move beyond one's comfort level to be stretched intellectually, culturally, and socially; however, before reaching this point, there are often economic, cultural, and social hurdles that must be overcome. These barriers define many of the challenges confronting our teachers every day. A family's economic situation may well affect a child's ability to be attentive in the classroom or even be present in class on a daily basis. Furthermore, family economics may influence a child's perception of fitting in with classmates who are perceived to have certain creature comforts.

School-age children are products of their family environments and everything that that encompasses. This reality can lead children to feel economically or socially inferior or superior, whichever applies. The result is a negative or positive effect on a child's potential for or interest in learning, because his or her level of interest or self-confidence is altered. Similarly, academics can be considered insignificant relative to a youth culture that celebrates the ability to be prosperous and successful outside of the path of academics. The prominence of music, fashion, and sports in the contemporary youth culture demands that educators interpret these elements of the youth world as a means toward understanding the relative impact of the culture on students' learning and interest levels. The preeminent concern today in many classrooms filled with underperforming and distracted school-age children is how to develop a consistent means of teaching that mitigates the economic, cultural, and social effects that are indelible in many of the children's lives.

In actuality, classroom teachers enter their profession with personalized views of the world, almost certain to be accompanied by definite sets of biases and prejudgments. The challenge is to allow oneself to be moved beyond one's own views and biases toward a view of the complexities of the world that is informed by others' ideas and experiences. To teach about the intricacies of our world, teaching professionals must appreciate, respect, and comprehend the diversity and multiplicity that characterize it. Only a mature, fair-minded professional of goodwill is able to check his or her prejudices at the classroom door to provide every student with the opportunities and tools to learn. Effective teaching is a reciprocal and organic process, and those who grasp this reality serve the students and the profession well.

Recruitment and retention. The education industry has been rather complacent in its efforts to restructure the recruitment and retention systems for classroom instructors. One consequence of this is the significant decline in the supply of qualified and interested teaching candidates. Our unwillingness (or lack of funding) to provide sufficient teaching resources and professional incentives has exacerbated this dilemma. Although most of us agree that teaching is one of the most important and revered vocations in our society, the reality is that we do not recognize or compensate teachers in a manner that reflects this consensus. Once we decide to view teaching as a true profession, then perhaps we will witness a major shift in not only the compensation levels but the quantity, quality, and commitment of persons choosing it as a preferred career choice. Teaching professionals are essentially stewards of children; they unlock the talents, gifts, and abilities inside of them. Through the genius, sensibilities, and dedication of teachers, young people begin to identify their unique talents and envision a world different from their own. The task before us is to recognize, encourage, and support our teaching professionals as they perform these sacred tasks.

We must devise new ways of sparking widespread interest in the profession to produce a new generation of committed and highly trained professionals. Specifically, there needs to be a renewed emphasis on achieving a more socially and culturally diverse corps of teachers who can interpret the conditions in which many of our youth live and play. Our children deserve professionals who can translate concepts and ideas into ways of learning that make sense in multiple contexts. Indeed, the ability to integrate young people's experiences with new concepts as a means toward learning requires creativity and flexibility. Further, the adaptability and insight necessary to provide effective learning environments for children is not taught in the academy alone but is developed through diverse life experiences and broad academic and professional training. Perhaps, the most visible initiative that has been developed to attract highly qualified teachers to teach in urban and rural schools is Wendy Kopp's Teach for America. Other efforts include the recruitment of military and business professionals to teach in public schools; some foundations are funding programs that accommodate the entry of these noneducation professionals into teaching.

Although teaching had enjoyed a place of prominence for decades as a preferred vocation, in the current marketplace it has to compete with numerous professions that offer more attractive salary and benefits packages as well as job prestige. Marketing and public relations for teachers occur on such a small scale that teaching gets drowned out by the other more visible and lucrative career options. A marketing pitch that combines a competitive salary and an attractive benefits package with the potential to nurture and shape young minds would seem to be a hard line to follow, especially given that many adults want to earn a decent living while making a difference in the world. (Note how the military has become active in promoting military service as a worthwhile career choice, as evidenced by its creative and captivating marketing campaigns via television and print advertisements.) Expanding teacher recruitment into areas not commonly aligned with teaching is precisely the type of marketing approach needed. Fresh perspectives from those not traditionally interested in classroom teaching can inject the new energy that is desperately needed in the profession.

As we expand how and where we recruit classroom teachers, we must look beyond the traditional pipelines and toward those professions and institutions that have access to broadly skilled individuals. Just as the business, medical, and legal professions recruit persons who possess academic and professional training that is relevant for success in their respective fields, the teaching profession must continue to insist that its recruits possess specific academic preparation as well as some form of advanced academic or professional experience. What is common among established professions is that, not only do their professionals possess specific knowledge and training about their work, but they also possess a broad academic base (usually, a liberal arts platform) as a foundation that is transferable across many careers. By collaborating with experienced human resource professionals in the business, medical, and legal professions, educators can begin to create precise expectations of the skills and abilities that are important for a teacher to be successful in the classroom. Other professions have been successful at recruiting highly and broadly skilled individuals who provide many benefits for the clientele and organizations that they serve. As elementary and secondary educators improve their capacity to identify, recruit, and retain highly trained teachers, a professionalization of teaching will occur, thus elevating the stature of the classroom teacher.

To attract the highly skilled and experienced persons that we need, the industry must engage in a comprehensive reassessment of the profession.

The increased expectations and requirements being attached to training and development programs will require full-scale compensation packages that reflect these higher standards. Compensation and incentive structures that reward instructors for succeeding in their work are long overdue. Although some justify the absence of teacher incentives by arguing the potential for abuse, there remains no legitimate reason for not establishing an effective means of compensating our teachers for meeting preestablished academic goals. There are not many professions in our industrialized society that do not reward their professionals for success in their work.

It is imperative that we reform our approach to teacher compensation as a means toward eliminating the double standards and hypocrisy that we have applied against the profession for so long. We judge them for not being effective in the classroom while we do not provide the means for them to be adequately trained through professional development programs. This type of schizophrenia has to cease because we are jeopardizing the academic and professional futures of our children. The restructuring of the compensation and professional development systems for teaching professionals should take place concurrently because both will facilitate our capacity to recruit and retain professionals who possess the ambition and commitment to serve our youth adequately.

The Partnership for New York City has explored ways to award teacher bonuses based on factors such as increased test scores and improved classroom attendance. The State of Massachusetts had proposed a plan that would link merit pay to classroom performance, as opposed to rewarding academic degrees and years of service. Incentive formats for teaching professionals can mirror bonus structures that are commonly utilized in the private sector. Preestablished sales quotas, stock prices, and cost reductions are the kinds of benchmarks being employed in private enterprise as a basis for employee incentives. As educators consider how and whether classroom teachers should be given bonuses or incentives, the behaviors and outcomes being awarded must be aligned with the primary goals of school-age education to mitigate the usual pitfalls surrounding incentive structures. The potential for employee abuse and manipulation of data, conflicts of interest, and disincentives are commonly associated with many incentive programs.

School Hardware and Software

Comprehensive systemic reform must account for the inadequacies in school hardware (i.e., school facilities) and software (i.e., classroom engineering and curriculum design) if it is going to address the range of processes integral to teaching and learning. Raising the standards for school buildings and classrooms can contribute greatly to creating effective teaching and learning spaces. The absence of regularly maintained and upgraded physical space and the utilization of classroom space that emulates a 20th-century format are factors that may cause the classroom atmosphere to be less conducive to adaptive learning. Similarly, the use of curricula that do not account for nor incorporate differences in learning styles and learning paces negatively affect the potential for student academic success. To produce elementary and secondary schools that offer every student ample opportunity for academic success, each component process must be elevated to accommodate the increased standards and assessments being applied to schools and their constituents. The simultaneous elevation of school buildings, classrooms, and curricula makes it easier to justify raising our expectations of and standards for students, teaching professionals, schools, and school systems. Without expending greater investment toward school hardware and software, the broader conversation surrounding accountability, standards, and testing is rendered meaningless.

School facilities. The importance of structurally sound and technologically advanced school buildings should not be underestimated in terms of their impact on the overall education process. Dilapidated and dysfunctional school buildings are unacceptable as learning spaces for school-age children. Young people should not be expected to achieve at a high level under physical conditions that do not provide adequate comfort, safety, and security. Similarly, teaching professionals cannot teach or educate students who are distracted by their inability to concentrate because of classroom discomforts or a dysfunctional school culture. To the extent that we expect young people to succeed academically, we must be committed to ensuring that the physical tools, systems, and structures are in place to help them achieve measurable degrees of classroom success. For instance, preparation for a highly technical and information-oriented world can take place only in technologically advanced classrooms. To address the 21st-century emphasis on information and technology in elementary and secondary education, school facilities must be able to accommodate the infrastructure needed to produce state-of-the-art, modern facilities. For students and teachers to access information in real time, school infrastructure must be capable of handling the requisite computer systems and networks. To facilitate classroom communication within and across schools (and even states or countries), school buildings need to be wired properly. We will not be able to prepare our young people for an advanced and complex world if we do not address the state of school hardware.

Although most observers acknowledge the need to invest billions of dollars toward the renovation of schools, the challenge for those charged with the task continues to be identifying the funding sources for such a monumental investment. The debate is no longer whether the overhaul is needed but whether public and private financing entities can create the financial strategies and plans to accomplish it. The range of social and economic priorities that require major financial attention makes the school financing issues even more daunting. The combination of public and private funding of elementary and secondary education will contribute to the realization of school renovations. Some of the creative means of financing these building upgrades include space sharing with community organizations, public bond issuances or equity offerings, donation of vacant buildings by municipalities and private owners, provision of below-market loans by financial institutions and community development corporations, usage of creative financial vehicles such as a sale–leaseback transaction, and direct investment by companies and individuals.

The costs associated with renovation of school facilities that have not been adequately maintained for several decades are so vast that the most economical approach is to build facilities that can be cross-utilized throughout a community. Social service organizations, schools, and community resource/recreational centers can be colocated in one large multipurpose facility that has space allocated for each of the school, social service, and community needs. Space sharing achieves economies of scale because it facilitates the financing of physical space that addresses a combination of community needs. The existence of old vacant buildings and lots is a hidden resource in many urban communities. Urban municipalities can donate these types of buildings at almost zero cost to the recipient, whereas private owners can receive a range of tax credits or incentives for contributing real estate toward education and other social service and community purposes. Financial enterprises and community development corporations can participate in facilities enhancements by offering grants or loans whose interest rates are below market. The provision of financial relief in the form of lower debt-servicing requirements will go a long way toward freeing up dollars for school operating costs in the annual budget. Another alternative for private companies is to provide direct investment, which can lead to tax incentives as a social investment or as a charitable contribution toward elementary and secondary education. One example of the financial vehicles available to schools that can help make buildings affordable in the short term is the use of a sale–leaseback facility. Massachusetts's finance and development authority, MassDevelopment, awarded more than $20 million to six charter schools to finance facilities projects. In New York City, the Schoolhouse Foundation has raised $200 million through bond issues to build school facilities.

Classroom reengineering and curriculum design. School software (i.e., classroom engineering and curriculum design) has a significant impact on young people's abilities to learn and teaching professionals' abilities to teach as much as any aspect of the education process. The adaptability of learning spaces and the curriculum can be key determinants of academic success. The traditional classroom layout, whereby the students sit in rows of desks and the teacher leads from the chalkboard, may not always represent the most effective mode of teaching and learning. One solution is to engineer learning spaces in a manner that is suitable for a professional's teaching style and capacity. The unique characteristics of a group of students may need to be incorporated in the design to tailor the setting to what is deemed suitable for their needs. Similarly, a standardized curriculum may serve as only a guideline for a classroom instructor, given that the breadth and content of some topics or lessons may warrant adaptations for particular contexts. Although this reality is acknowledged by many educators, many other situations exist wherein a standardized curriculum is essentially being forced to fit. Adaptability, creativity, and flexibility must be the driving forces in front of classroom engineering and curriculum design. We must be careful not to compromise our expectations of the students but to ensure that we are developing effective formats and formulas that accompany high academic standards while producing high academic achievement.

Classroom settings that are organic, interactive, and integrative can elicit the academic productivity that we are seeking from our students. Allowing usage of different classroom formats can very well lead us to a rebirth in the overall academic achievement of school-age children. Perhaps the most agreed-on aspect of classroom engineering is the view that smaller classroom sizes are ideal. Indeed, this facilitates and enhances the degree and quality of interaction between students and teachers, as well as that among the students themselves. In those situations where it is not necessarily feasible to decrease the size of the classroom, we must devise alternative approaches or layouts that will enable similar degrees of interaction and subsequent learning. The incorporation of subgroups within large classrooms and the utilization of paraprofessionals to assist with these groups can continue to be a workable alternative. Alternating classroom schedules by days and times is already a solution for many practitioners burdened by large classroom sizes.

A separate dimension to consider when reengineering classrooms is how to effectively create integrative formats such as cross-age, cross-grade, and cross-subject classrooms that can engender academic success across ages and stages of development. The recognition by many elementary and secondary practitioners of the varying learning paces and stages of school-age children has allowed parents and students to tailor the students' abilities to the range of subjects being offered. These cross-dimensional approaches create opportunities for young people to learn from their peers as they develop and mature at an individualized pace. We must avoid the temptation to track students into predetermined learning categories, by allowing sufficient flexibility in the programs that we offer them.

The integration of technology into classrooms is a major piece of the reengineering process because this component of teaching and learning will require teachers and students to utilize video, voice, and data devices in ways that may not be customary or easily interpreted. It is the joint responsibility of the administrators and the teaching professionals to devise effective means of integrating technology into classroom activities as well as into administrative and operational functions. Many technology professionals are willing and committed to instructing elementary and secondary educators on how to effectively utilize the best of technological applications in the education of tomorrow's leaders. The potential for these tools is vast and unlimited and essentially opens up the world to school-age children as they explore and unlock their own academic interests and intellectual pursuits.

The focus of any comprehensive curriculum ought to be to accommodate the varied learning styles, challenges, and paces of children across grade and age levels. Although a fully customized or tailored instructional program is most likely not feasible because of financial and logistical constraints, a broader attempt at developing curriculum formats that respond to different learning needs is always warranted. Accomplishing this time-intensive goal will require creativity and insight on the part of the classroom teacher to develop curricula that fit a range of learning styles. For decades, we have failed our children because we have incorrectly imposed a certain learning style on them, and we have failed to design curricula and classroom activities around their particular needs. We have enough evidence to know that one size does not fit all students as it pertains to how they learn.

The biggest and most challenging aspect of curriculum design seems to be accommodating the different learning paces of students in one classroom. Related to this is the difficulty in identifying and managing the learning differences that accompany the different paces. Traditionally, educators have simply lumped "slow" learners into "special-needs" classes or just ignored their learning needs altogether. In many instances, learning differences and learning challenges have been inappropriately labeled as behavioral problems or learning deficiencies, which has subsequently led to students being placed inappropriately in special-needs classes. Our inability to properly identify or distinguish learning differences and challenges has resulted in the greatest educational failure and disservice in the history of elementary and secondary education. The reality is that every child learns differently and some children require greater attention. This does not always reflect the need for special-needs classes but does sometimes represent the need for greater creativity and awareness by the classroom teacher. The easy and unimaginative response to learning differences has been to place students in special-needs classes, whereas the responsible and ethical approach to teaching students who learn differently is to design the curriculum in a manner that accommodates a range of learning styles and paces. Truly meaningful curriculum design requires commitment and effort from educators; otherwise, we will continue this spiral of falling academic performance from our youth.

Curriculum content has always been and continues to be debatable. Indeed, topics and subjects covered in 20th-century classrooms are not necessarily relevant today, in and of themselves. Although many topics in literature, history, mathematics, and science are timeless in their application, they should be broadened to expose dimensions that may have been omitted in the past. As related to literature and history, there are innumerable writers, stories, and historical experiences that need to be exposed as we educate our youth. With the advent of technology, enhancing the content has become even less burdensome. Teaching and learning math and science topics has changed dramatically with the application of technology. The teaching professional's ability to present content that is meaningful to the experiences and ideas of an array of events and groups is a determining factor in how relevant a curriculum plan is deemed from the perspectives of a range of stakeholders.

A separate focus is how to effectively integrate curricula across subjects, age groups, and grades, as a means toward producing an educational continuum that can be applied throughout a student's elementary and secondary tenure. The existence of differences in learning styles and paces presents unique challenges for the development of a continuum. If a generalized curriculum plan can be designed that identifies successive topics, subjects, aptitudes, and skills by learning stages (as opposed to grade levels), then an individualized educational continuum can follow such a plan. This is similar to what we currently identify as those skills that should be developed at certain ages. The goal is not to place students in categories but to devise a plan that enables each student to acquire specific and broad skills and aptitudes by high school graduation. Addendums to any type of educational continuum require us to manage learning deficiencies through the usage of extra classroom sessions and teaching specialists.

3

BENEFITS OF CROSS-SECTORAL COLLABORATION

A *Call to the Village* is intended to lead the way for individuals and institutions of the nonprofit, private, public, and religious sectors as they engage themselves, their resources, and the communities in the development of collaborative strategies for transforming local schools. As citizens across the nation ponder how and what to do about the state of public education, cross-sectoral collaboration (CSC) will provide numerous alternatives for improving community schools. This collaborative framework is timely and relevant because it acknowledges the distinctiveness of the entities that compose each sector, and it delineates for them how they can translate their distinctive competencies into innovative education collaboratives. This strategic guide is unique because it not only encourages partnerships and collaboration but also facilitates the infusion of diverse voices and new ideas in school reform initiatives. CSC distinguishes itself by

- drawing distinctions across the nonprofit, private, public, and religious sectors and delineating their respective roles in school reform;
- presenting a strategic framework that is a viable means for building effective partnerships across sectors;

- identifying each sector's distinctive competencies as they emanate from each sector's routine strengths and proficiencies; and
- establishing a platform for professionals and sectors to engage one another around innovative ideas and perspectives pertaining to public school transformation

By advocating partnerships, this collaborative framework seeks to create avenues for firms and people to exhibit their interests in and fulfill their commitment to local school improvements. This guide enables prospective partners to develop options derived from their unique experiences and perspectives. An implicit goal of the framework is for participants to devise solutions that build from existing assets, skills, and expertise, in a manner that corresponds with the established priorities of the partnering organizations. The foundation of CSC relates to partners' abilities to create educational prototypes that will incorporate resources already being utilized in their daily operations. This book exposes an infinite number of ways in which collaborative ventures will allow organizations to achieve multiple objectives concurrently without investing substantially more human, physical, or financial resources.

CSC separates itself from other propositions by focusing on the creation of strategic partnerships that make sense in the context of what each sector has to offer. It does not examine collaborative opportunities through one lens; instead, it isolates the sectors and extrapolates their unique opportunities based on proprietary or customary expertise and resources. It exposes administrative, managerial, pedagogical, technical, and operational opportunities within public education that can be aligned with the various specializations of the nonprofit, private, public, and religious sectors and the organizations that form these sectors. The community networks and tailored programs that are customarily employed by local nonprofits can be useful for a school collaborative attempting to solicit external contributions from a community for student extracurricular activities. Similarly, many financial and operational systems that enjoy widespread use in private companies are transferable to local school settings as a means toward improving school management and operations. The underutilized physical space held by some large churches can be a viable solution to the space constraints being experienced by school administrators and teaching professionals.

CSC is a workable alternative for improving elementary and secondary education and for providing a forum for persons and organizations from the different sectors, industries, and professions to collaborate around education reform. It has significant potential for improving how we educate our youth because it enables the integration of innovative ideas in setting education policies and strategies. Beyond what it portends for education, CSC has the potential to build bridges across sectors that can ultimately transform how we fulfill our organizational and sectoral mandates in the years ahead. Although the primary advantages of this framework relate to its capacity to produce effective school prototypes and innovative teaching and learning methodologies, it can significantly affect how firms and individuals share information and resources while developing effective partnerships for improving schools.

The information and resource exchange that CSC engenders across the sectors can lead to greater efficiencies and increased cost-effectiveness for entities that do not tend to have extravagant amounts of time and resources at their disposal. Because most organizations do not operate with substantial capital reserves or discretionary funds, any proposal that is designed to solicit participation in external ventures such as CSC would need to require minimal levels of financial or human resource investment. Entities participating in a collaborative approach can conceivably experience organizational benefits without expending one additional dollar. For instance, many firms will be able to dedicate employees' time to a school on a pro bono basis to assist in specialized areas, such as computer support by a technology firm or dramatic-arts lessons by a local theater company. By establishing a school collaborative as the designated charitable program for a specified period, firms might be in a better position to persuade their workers to get involved in external activities or capital campaigns. In this type of situation, firms are often able to achieve their philanthropic goals without expending financial resources. Although collaborative efforts may begin with the mere intent of information and resource exchange, they can lead to the realization of many efficiencies and opportunities for organizational growth and exposure.

CSC BENEFITS DEFINED

Some of the tangible benefits to be gained from participation in partnerships include improved effectiveness and efficiencies, economies of scale, organizational synergies, cross-utilization of resources, and transferability of skills and assets. As firms consider ways of substantiating investments in products, services, and systems (i.e., achieving a greater bang for the buck), the potential benefits from CSC participation can cause investment decisions to make even better strategic and financial sense. Increased utilization of systems, expansion of marketing and distribution channels, development of new uses for sunk costs, and increased customer base represent the types of opportunities in public education that can improve the effectiveness, efficiencies, economies, and synergies for an enterprise.

A nonprofit enterprise that has a strong service record of providing nontraditional products and services to underserved markets can use its local knowledge and experience to assist schools with developing strategic programs for specific student populations. Because so many local nonprofit organizations understand the impact of factors such as high levels of crime and unemployment on the viability of a community, they can use this accumulated expertise in a collaborative to assist educators in the development of teaching and learning modules aimed at youth whose environments are affected by these kinds of social and economic factors. A major challenge for teaching professionals is how to effectively teach students whose lives are affected by negative externalities in their homes and neighborhoods. A nonprofit that contributes in this way enhances the utilization of some of its proprietary resources and achieves greater efficiencies by being able to channel its accumulated expertise into the development of solutions to address the learning needs of targeted student groups.

A major corporation that has invested heavily in technology systems that improve how it monitors the operations and activities of subsidiaries around the world might be able to apply this same technology to a local school or school district as a way of helping to develop better ways of evaluating the performance of different components of the school operations or even how schools compare in areas such as reading or math. The mere application of sunk technology costs into unanticipated programs such as public education are the kinds of untapped opportunities that firms and professionals from all sectors can expect to encounter as they collaborate. A prominent mandate confronting school administrators under the current political climate is to establish effective means of communicating how schools and school systems are performing vis-à-vis standardized benchmarks for specific grade levels. The need to upgrade existing evaluation systems and methods, as well as the need for more clarity in the interpretation of the measurements and outcomes, reflects opportunities for private companies to engage public educators in discussions about the application of technology as a means toward achieving more consistent and reliable data as they relate to student academic performance.

Public enterprises that operate at the state and local levels have acquired fundamental knowledge about their respective student populations that has not always been readily available to public entities at the federal level. One of the real advantages held by the public sector is its educational expertise related to defining the critical stages and elements of elementary and secondary education. Organizations that are responsible for overseeing school systems at the local and state levels possess indispensable knowledge and experience that would undoubtedly be advantageous to a collaborative. This sector's ability to bring its expertise to a venture that includes partners from other sectors can ensure that the integrity of school-age education remains at the core of an endeavor. In this way, public educators would be able to spread their educational resources across more programs and apply their know-how to innovative school prototypes being offered by noneducation organizations that may not possess the requisite expertise related to schools.

The community leadership and influence that is often associated with the religious sector and its leaders can be extremely beneficial in a collaborative. Because so many religious entities are consistently challenged by the need to respond to so many ministerial needs with a limited operating budget, their ability to influence and lead a community without dipping into limited funds would be a crucial advantage as it pertains to CSC involvement. The essence of participation in CSC is not at all tied to how much financial investment a partner can make; instead, it is primarily related to how well partners are able to identify the needs of local schools and develop meaningful solutions to these problems based on the unique contributions and expertise of the participating entities. This reality defines why CSC is different from other proposals; it acknowledges that there are clearly identifiable contributions that each sector can make toward enhancing public schools in local communities. The intangible assets that religious organizations wield in their surrounding communities reflect the essence of CSC. This sector's participation can often be linked to its prominence and service in the minds of the constituents.

Enhancing organizational effectiveness and efficiencies are almost always primary concerns for organizations that are charged with meeting multiple objectives of competing stakeholder groups. Whether the goal is to spread a fixed level of resources across more units or to increase expected outcomes from a static level of input, the challenge is consistently how to produce greater return from a fixed investment of some sort. CSC can assist firms and individuals with meeting these kinds of objectives because the fundamental premise of the framework is to develop means by which partners can utilize existing resources or systems to improve the administrative, operational, teaching, and learning processes within local schools. By definition, this collaborative approach is intended to aid participating firms and individuals in achieving greater effectiveness and efficiencies by expanding the utility of assets and investments that have already been dedicated in some way, not by expending additional or unsubstantiated resources. Current economic and political conditions as well as impending climates reinforce the need to provide CSC participants with options that have minimal financial investments attached.

The translation of organizational distinctive competencies into scenarios that would add value to schools will allow participating entities to transfer skills or assets into strategically defined areas of school-age education. For example, a family and children's services organization whose expertise is addressing domestic challenges can allow its staff to collaborate with classroom teachers in managing the effects of these issues on students' capacities to learn. A foundation that has a strong record of fund-raising can collaborate with local school and district administrators to design creative fund-raising strategies aimed at supplementing school operating budgets. Separately, dedicating idle physical space for use as a school facility has the effect of yielding unanticipated benefits from an investment that may have once been a nonproducing asset. Similarly, the cross-utilization of a firm's professionals as mentors for pro bono work in a neighborhood school produces meaningful exchange and dialogue between students and professionals without the incurrence of additional compensation costs. As entities from every sector contemplate strategies for contributing to public education, CSC provides them with viable options that enable the integration of local school needs with the distinctive competencies of organizations.

Many existing entrepreneurial ventures are exposing varied scenarios for improving how schools operate, how teachers teach, and how children learn through the application of products, services, and systems that are customarily employed by enterprises outside of the education industry. The adaptability of software packages or technology to classroom activities can lead to unexpected economies for the developers of the technology as well as for the student recipients. Certain management and operational systems of private corporations can be cross-utilized in local schools to achieve greater economies of scale as they relate to the reporting and monitoring needs of schools. Religious institutions that are seeking to expand their ministries into education initiatives may discover that their underutilized facilities can be transformed into an actual elementary school or into ancillary programs such as after-school tutoring or a Saturday arts curriculum.

Collaboration between individuals and institutions to transform the conditions of schools can be viewed as a springboard for developing new partners and prospects that can ultimately increase customer bases and service areas. An important element of CSC is that partners can produce organizational synergies in conjunction with the development of practicable solutions to school dilemmas. For example, a collaborative that includes a foundation and a private corporation can conceivably lead to the formation of a long-standing partnership between two entities that are committed to elementary and secondary education. The corporation might represent a new funding source for the foundation, or, conversely, the foundation can be the means by which the corporation is able to maintain an ongoing presence as a key player in philanthropic initiatives targeted at school-age education. Similarly, a collaborative that consists of a church and a community development financial institution can be the basis for a new financial relationship that enables the church to expand its ministerial reach and that provides the financial institution with a new client and greater visibility in a community. Although organizational synergies can translate into benefits as basic as sharing markets or marketing to each other's customers, the potential within CSC extends well beyond the partners' contributions to school reform.

DISTINCTIVE COMPETENCIES OF THE SECTORS

CSC is unique because it identifies opportunities in education for individuals and institutions. Building from the routine operations and expertise of the sectors, the framework establishes strategic alternatives to be used as guides for their respective participation in CSC. By defining the nonprofit, private, public, and religious sectors based on fundamental similarities and consistencies across their member entities, this strategic guide offers workable strategies to follow for improving local schools. The intent is not to constrain particular firms and persons to a fixed set of strategic options; instead, the purpose is to propose diverse solutions to school reform for entities that have not traditionally been involved in public school decision making. As these organizations strategize about how to make schools largely effective once again, the hope is that they will realize the value that they carry individually and collectively as unique enterprises.

CSC acknowledges that the sectors are not necessarily mutually exclusive, meaning that some entities can be considered hybrid organizations that are categorized as members of more than one sector. For instance, although private foundations tend to be accountable to families, trusts, and other private interests, disassociating them from the core emphasis of their work is difficult, given that it often mirrors the social and public service activities of nonprofits. Colleges and universities can be characterized as public or private institutions; however, most of them carry a tax-exempt status as a nonprofit. Similarly, the activities of church subsidiaries are most likely to have a social service or economic focus, but their parent organizations are members of the religious sector. For the sake of simplicity, foundations and postsecondary educational institutions will be associated with the nonprofit sector, and church tax-exempt subsidiaries will be linked to the religious sector.

When one considers the role of religious institutions in public education reform, the mandate for the separation of church and state comes immediately to mind. Just as the church–state doctrine essentially forbids any application of public funds in a way that would advocate a particular religion, CSC does not advocate or propose that religious-sector participation involve any attempt to compromise the neutrality and objectivity of public education. Within CSC, the expected roles of religious organizations have nothing to do with the possibility of influencing school curricula or any other educational component that rightfully resides within the domain of public school administrators and teaching professionals. This sector's unique potential in school reform relates primarily to the prominence, influence, access, and stature wielded by religious entities and their leaders in local communities. Indeed, there are innumerable scenarios by which the sector can play a vital role in improving community schools; however, none of these possibilities will jeopardize the constitutional mandate for maintaining a separation of church and state.

The distinctive competencies of religious institutions emanate from their role as a type of moral or spiritual guide for the members of their churches, temples, mosques, and synagogues, as well as for citizens of the surrounding communities. Because of their involvement with nurturing the human spirit and ministering to the spiritual needs of parishioners, religious institutions are endowed with a great deal of reverence and trust by those being guided and served. This reality establishes these entities as influencing how people live their lives and make daily decisions pertaining to family, school, and work. Building from their unique influence on and access to large numbers of citizens in a community, churches, synagogues, and so forth, can prove to be abiding forces in a collaborative effort. Their spiritual and moral authority can be meaningful in terms of being able to convey goals of a new initiative to citizens of a community. People often seek guidance and explication about secular matters from those whom they trust and revere. As public schools continue to experiment with innovation on so many levels and engage nontraditional partners in the delivery of education, individuals and communities will rely on religious leadership to provide relevant information and direction that will assist them in making good choices for their children's education.

Related to the moral authority that is attached to religious leadership is the ability to interpret and explain in a manner that can lead to consensus and practicable strategies and solutions for students, schools, and communities. Although religious leaders possess their own views and beliefs about certain issues, their insistence on established principles and objectivity can instill a sense of good judgment and fairness into a collaborative and lead to alternatives that reflect partners' special contributions and students' special needs. As a type of community liaison, religious institutions can play a vital role in not only leading an initiative but also mitigating differing views among diverse stakeholders within a community. Similar to the average citizen, persons and organizations representing the nonprofit, private, and public sectors possess a healthy level of reverence for religious leaders and their perspectives on many social and public issues. The mere presence of such moral clout defines one of the more distinct advantages that religious institutions can bring to CSC.

An evolving advantage of many members of the religious community is the growing investment in substantial physical assets. The megachurch phenomenon has resulted in the acquisition and development of multiple acres of land by churches that view these expansion strategies as being relevant to their overall emphasis on comprehensive ministries. The need to provide programs and activities that address social, recreational, spiritual, and various other personal needs has been the impetus behind this movement. Although much of the physical space is primarily utilized during the weekends, there are real opportunities for space sharing with local social service providers and for the development of school-age activities, such as after-school, weekend, and summer programs. An even more ambitious possibility is to charter a school prototype on the premises. Depending on the vision and tolerance of the leadership, any church or similar entity can lead in improving school conditions for youth in surrounding neighborhoods by dedicating underutilized physical space to accommodate a school or conduct ancillary educational activities.

The religious sector is also well positioned in local communities because of an increasing willingness to engage in ministerial pursuits that extend beyond church pulpits and traditional boundaries. Whether driven by the inadequacies of private and other social enterprises or their own expanded missions to address secular challenges confronting parishioners, churches are doing more to meet a multiplicity of member needs. As churches participate more in community and economic development projects, they are discovering new partners from each of the sectors. Banks have been willing to collaborate and do joint ventures with churches as a means of enhancing their customer base as well as to fulfill mandates within community reinvestment legislation. Nonprofits have found local partners to assist in building sustainable and productive community institutions. Federal and state governmental agencies have rediscovered that churches and other religious entities can be key players in the administration of public initiatives in local areas. By expanding their ministerial agendas, religious institutions have paved the way for the creation of multidimensional collaborations with the nonprofit, private, and public sectors. Their ability to lead cross-sectoral partnerships that address economic and social issues should enable religious entities to provide similar leadership within CSC in education.

The competencies of the nonprofit sector relate to the organizations' proximity to the clientele and to the local knowledge acquired about neighborhoods and groups within their service areas. This sector's knowledge about micro-issues and concerns of a local community can be invaluable within CSC as partner organizations attempt to devise strategies for groups within a school community. Identifying historical, social, economic, and cultural factors that may affect school-age children reflects how important nonprofit partners can be in an education collaborative. Because the framework is designed to transform school processes and systems in ways that will respond to the special challenges of targeted communities, it will be crucial for organizations to know as much data as possible. This sector's experiences with citizens and groups within local markets, as well as its established record for delivering relevant goods and services, can be extremely beneficial to a collaborative as it develops solutions to public school dilemmas that may be unique to neighborhoods or segments within a population.

The nonprofit community's ability to provide customized products and programs for sections of a market has allowed it to fill economic and social gaps that have been the result of inadequacies in the private and public sectors. The work of foundations, social service providers, and community development corporations at local and state levels continues to prove that the role of nonprofits in the development and sustainability of neighborhoods is an invaluable one. Their provision of housing, medical care, job training, child care, family services, and investment opportunities reflect the broad array of community needs being addressed by the sector. This kind of familiarity with developing solutions to citizens' everyday needs at a microlevel provides a good foundation for a collaboration that is attempting to translate school and student needs into educational alternatives that make sense in particular contexts. Nonprofits' know-how pertaining to targeted markets should lessen the obstacles of understanding and defining multiple segments and populations in a specified area. Having worked with communities and their key constituencies, nonprofit organizations will be uniquely positioned to inform collaborative partners about these relationships and networks.

The nonprofit sector's role as a type of local barometer cannot be underestimated, especially in light of the intense obstacles that entrepreneurs and private companies face as they present their proposals to school systems regarding how schools can be improved. Some of the more formidable voices of opposition have come from community groups that have a history of challenging outsiders. Trusted and tested community institutions can be vital intermediaries under these kinds of conditions. An advantage of CSC is that it encourages private companies and entrepreneurs to collaborate with entities such as nonprofits and local churches as a means of mitigating the forces of opposition with which many have been confronted to date when offering new initiatives to school districts and communities. By partnering with local nonprofits, not only do the other sectors gain relevant knowledge and access that may not have been available otherwise, but they also win over reputable community institutions as advocates for their school plans and propositions.

Established local institutions can be key partners to have when entering new territories or markets. Nonprofits' relationships and networks within communities, in addition to their market know-how, define what are perhaps their greatest distinctive competencies for collaboration in the education industry. Being familiar with and aware of the critical stakeholder groups within a community can be a real advantage for outside organizations or individuals who have innovative plans for reforming schools in a community. Knowing these groups' particular interests and priorities as they relate to school issues can provide enormous insight into what plans would make the most sense and how to develop them. CSC acknowledges the benefits of having established community institutions on one's side, as opposed to entering a market without any advocates from the inside. Community stakeholders are more willing to trust the proposals of an outside party on the recommendation of a nonprofit with which they are accustomed to working.

The nonprofit sector is increasingly positioning itself as being complementary to the work of the private and public sectors. Without the programs of nonprofits, many citizens would simply not enjoy the benefits of owning a home, receiving sufficient medical care, or shopping at a neighborhood supermarket. Private-sector companies have not been as effective as nonprofits in meeting certain needs of some market segments because of preestablished financial guidelines, risk tolerance parameters, and even capital market concerns. Private-sector mandates such as profit maximization, cost-effectiveness, and increasing shareholder value limit the extent to which private companies can offer some of the specialized products and services provided by nonprofits. Public-sector entities have not been as successful as nonprofits, in part because of their limited capacities to fund programs that respond to needs at local and state levels. These gaps in state funding are being filled by nonprofit interventions. The public sector's perennial problems with implementation at the state and local levels continue to hamper the outcomes of many public initiatives. These realities underscore the importance of this sector's work and its commitment to reaching those markets that are not always adequately served. Nonprofit organizations' commitment to markets that are traditionally unserved or underserved can benefit a collaborative as the partners attempt to respond to those students and schools that have been neglected or poorly served themselves.

The private sector's ability to produce, market, and distribute products and services in ways that achieve measurable efficiencies and economies is an essential distinction between private enterprise and other organizational types. For many successful private companies, the application of systems, structures, and processes that integrate strategic and financial priorities facilitates their ongoing productivity and profitability. As a result of their building effective management, marketing, distribution, and financial systems, entities have been able to make better decisions, achieve operational efficiencies, and produce the necessary financial gains. The additional pressures to maximize profits, increase shareholder value, and maintain solvency force private entities and entrepreneurs to incorporate systems and tools that result in efficient allocation of resources as well as optimal investment and marketing strategies. In many ways, the external pressures applied by customers, stockholders, and competitors unintentionally compel private companies to adhere to financially strong and strategically sound decision making in all aspects of their business activities.

Although there are numerous levels of oversight and review being employed to monitor the academic performance of students and schools, the scrutiny has not historically led to corrections and restructurings that have produced strong academic records from the majority of students and schools. Appropriate systems and processes need to be developed and incorporated into the routine operations of schools and school systems to produce higher levels of achievement. By collaborating with private-industry professionals, public educators can design processes for classrooms and schools that will provide insight regarding how well or not students are learning and teachers are teaching. There is a great need in education for evaluation methods that identify specifics about students' academic performance, as opposed to simplistic and broad summaries about categories of learning. One of the primary opportunities in education for private-sector companies is leading public educators in the design of systems that will produce meaningful data and information in the proper contexts. Educators can gain tremendous insight from practitioners who have been successful at obtaining all kinds of sales, financial, and marketing data from internally produced systems that are useful in the ongoing management and evaluation of the operations of an enterprise.

As advocates on both sides of the debate argue whether private companies should be allowed to participate in the delivery of public education, the reality is that the focus ought to be shifted to how to effectively utilize the best practices, resources, and expertise of private enterprise in reengineering public school classrooms, structures, and systems. A critical step toward applying private-sector models to public education is to implement mechanisms that will produce meaningful data and information to assist educators in understanding the nature of teaching and learning weaknesses as well as strengths. Many existing models seem to provide generalized data that do very little in terms of pinpointing the academic needs for individual students. Private-sector professionals routinely design computer models and programs that measure those parameters deemed critical for specific kinds of strategic, operational, or marketing decisions. This degree of microanalysis and specificity in evaluation models is missing in public school accountability initiatives. By partnering with private-sector professionals, educators can invent proprietary models that will provide more precise data pertaining to student academic needs, and they can learn how to use the data to reinvent teaching and learning activities.

The integration of computer technology in more aspects of public school operations can transform how administrators manage their schools, how teachers teach in the classroom, and how students learn. As many school systems are discovering, a comprehensive approach to the employment of technology has tremendous operational and administrative advantages. Electronic formats allow administrators to view the academic progress of classes and examine expenditures across schools in real time, whereas teachers can communicate with parents throughout the day regarding any range of student issues. The integration of computer software as a learning tool has already proven to educators how critical it is for elementary and secondary students to grasp computer-oriented learning. Computer professionals possess the expertise that educators can tap into to assist in the development of software and programs that can be effective in improving how administrators and teachers perform their tasks daily. CSC will enable the collaboration between computer specialists and educators as they devise efficient electronic formats that will enhance the ongoing management and operations of classrooms and schools.

One prominent characteristic of private companies is their consistent emphasis on measuring inputs and outcomes in most aspects of their operations, albeit sometimes at the expense of important priorities such as client development or customer service. Their results orientation not only allows them to monitor the progress of their operations but also provides them with the information needed to redistribute or shift resources along the way. Although the private sector has been commonly criticized for its bottom-line focus, without such emphasis one can surely contend that private entrepreneurs and firms would not be as effective or efficient. Public education can benefit from the incorporation of reporting tools that enable the ongoing monitoring of student academic progress and administrative matters. Similar to the tools being implemented in many academic settings to accommodate the trend toward testing and accountability, adequate monitoring and reporting systems can be tremendously beneficial when the goal is to track thousands of students and schools. The existing emphasis in the industry on test scores and performance indicators has exposed a range of scenarios in which public educators, private companies, and entrepreneurs can collaborate to develop evaluation and reporting systems to monitor the academic achievement of students, as well as the regular operations and management of schools and school districts.

An important distinctive competence of the public sector is that its member organizations oversee and administer education policies, standards, practices, and guidelines. As the chief managers of elementary and secondary schools, public institutions and administrators possess substantial experience and knowledge pertaining to the intricacies of school-age education. This sector's know-how is unmatched as it relates to analyzing and interpreting microtopics in education. Their expertise in areas such as curriculum development, teacher training, classroom pedagogy, special-needs learning, testing, and so on, is vital and should serve as the technical basis for any experiment in CSC. CSC affirms this indispensable knowledge that public-sector institutions and professionals have acquired, and it acknowledges that there are numerous untapped resources throughout the other sectors that can be combined with public-sector know-how, surely leading to meaningful enhancements in public schools. Partnerships among persons and organizations of the nonprofit, private, public, and religious sectors can lead to innovative education prototypes that incorporate some of the best practices and tools of each of the sectors.

The areas of expertise that have been accumulated by public educators can be the essential technical guide needed by cocollaborators who have little or no exposure to the detailed elements of teaching school-age children. Experienced classroom instructors can offer input regarding optimal classroom sizes by grade level or age group. Seasoned administrators will know whether it makes sense to outsource student transportation services or facilities management. The combination of public-sector education knowledge and private-sector management proficiency can produce school management systems that yield improved operational efficiencies. Collaboration between social service professionals of the nonprofit sector and classroom teachers can improve how some of the nonacademic challenges are managed in the classroom. By partnering with local churches, music and art instructors can secure facilities to house after-school or weekend programs in these areas. For the sectors to create meaningful solutions to local school dilemmas, they will need to rely on the competencies and experiences of public-sector education professionals.

Aside from their areas of training and proficiency, public-sector professionals at local and state levels have the advantage of being able to monitor student progress. Although many of the evaluation systems lack comprehensiveness, education officials do maintain the basic capabilities to monitor student achievement vis-à-vis preestablished standards by grade level or age. As they assess students' progress in each academic area and across grades, teachers and administrators develop overall conclusions about student learning needs and successes. These kinds of assessments can provide invaluable data for cocollaborators as they strategize about the nature of proposed solutions to challenges confronting schools in targeted communities. In a situation where collaborators have determined that an overall reconfiguration of classrooms is appropriate, data pertaining to student achievement can be useful for placing students in certain classes. Similarly, if ongoing monitoring efforts indicate that students in targeted schools may be underachieving in some academic areas, then intervention by collaborators can be channeled where there is the greatest amount of academic need.

Local and state education entities also serve as useful implementers of federal education programs that are targeted at specific markets or skill development areas. The delivery and funding gaps between the appropriations for federal education initiatives and their actual implementation continue to require local intervention to ensure that the goals of the initiatives are not completely ignored. Similar to nonprofit organizations, local and state public entities are closer to local markets and have established networks and relationships with notable individuals and institutions locally. This allows them to know about the details for specific populations and have access to particular segments of communities. The logistical and administrative challenges that often accompany new federal education mandates necessitate the involvement of state and local organizations; otherwise, the mandates could not be implemented or managed properly.

Collaboration among federal, state, and local education officials has consistently enabled the dissemination and enforcement of critical education imperatives.

The substantial funding capacity at the federal government level is a huge advantage for this sector. As the ultimate overseer and provider of public education, the federal government has the responsibility to sufficiently fund its education priorities. Unfortunately, the perennial complaint is that federal allocations are not adequate for administering the requisite education programs. Public-sector entities at all levels significantly affect the amount of money that school districts have to expend on inventive programs. Most of the original solutions for transforming schools are funded at the federal level or through partnerships with the private sector because most state budgets typically cannot handle all of the costs associated with education innovation at the elementary and secondary levels. States depend on federal appropriations or external funding from private companies, foundations, and entrepreneurs to supplement their education budgets and subsidize new initiatives. Access to sizable financial resources can lessen the financial burden of any venture, especially when available resources from cocollaborators are already limited. The public sector's ability to channel legislative appropriations toward particular local collaborative models can be a huge victory for all sides.

CSC can be a useful alternative for rural, suburban, and urban school communities. Although the breadth of resources and organizational participation will likely vary across the different contexts, the potential benefits of collaboration remain accessible to schools and school systems of all sizes. To minimize a disproportionate allocation of financial, human, and organizational resources, school systems of varying sizes and contexts should work to collaborate beyond their customary boundaries. State and local school administrators can assist with ensuring a more equitable approach to building partnerships across industries, professions, and sectors. By encouraging partnerships throughout states and across sectors and localities, school administrators allow schools in isolated rural areas, as well as those in suburban and urban environments, to gain from some of the best practices and systems of the nonprofit, private, public, and religious sectors.

4

IMPLEMENTATION CHALLENGES AND REALITIES

The development, implementation, and management of a collaborative effort cannot occur without acknowledging and addressing the range of obstacles that have consistently hindered organizational partnerships in the past. CSC requires its participants to move beyond institutional and sectoral constraints to create means for ensuring the success of a collaborative. By effectively navigating the logistical, structural, organizational, political, and cultural terrains, participants can move closer to realizing many of the real advantages of CSC in education. For example, the partners' abilities to integrate nontraditional systems in local schools might prove to be a daunting task in communities where there may be a strong affinity for the status quo as it relates to public schools. By carefully managing the interests of each stakeholder group and illustrating in concrete terms the benefits of proposed systems, collaborators can enhance a community's acceptance of change. An organization that has operations in multiple states may discover that its participation in local-market school reform might carry different political consequences across the states that form its operating portfolio. Being able to explicate how school reform initiatives make overall strategic sense for the combined entity can help to mollify group tendencies to view philanthropic activities in political terms. Although one cannot realistically expect that the usual tensions and complexities across professions and industries will disappear, the hope is that the goals of CSC and its corresponding effects on school-age education will lead collaborators toward a heightened sense of commitment and persistence.

Often, the most difficult aspect of change is implementation or delivery at the various stages of a reform effort. Identifying potential implementation gaps as well as properly planning the execution process can go a long way toward achieving expected outcomes. Although certain teaching and learning programs may have produced strong results in some school settings, there is no guarantee that the same formats will produce similar results in other locations. Similarly, the availability of or accessibility to certain types of support and resources in some communities can be the determining factors for achieving timely implementation. Being able to rely on the expertise and experience of persons and organizations that already utilize programs being implemented in targeted schools is a real advantage. Anticipating political and cultural reactions to a firm's charitable activities can help define the nature and extent of participation in CSC or any public school reform project. Although any casual observer would agree that most firms and persons share a vested interest in ensuring that public schools and students perform at the highest academic levels, the reality is that there are varying schools of thought as to how this ideal can be achieved. Managing disparate interests of critical stakeholder groups must be done in ways that are inclusive of the diverse ideas that constituents may hold. In large, diverse organizations, this objective may be accomplished by engaging in multiple efforts that accomplish a broad spectrum of philanthropic objectives.

Preexisting motives and competing agendas held by stakeholder groups can strongly affect plan execution and seriously impede a collaborative venture. Firms and individuals' inabilities to work collaboratively have been derailed by the insistence on linking organizational participation to certain political or social interests, partners' unwillingness to compromise, an inability to fulfill a financial promise, a lack of strategic focus, and even the absence of enough committed partners to execute a planned initiative. Ideally, prospective CSC partners will not be deterred by the difficulties of past collaborative work but will instead be motivated by the potential to improve educational opportunities for young people. If collaborators can minimize the potential negative impact of the kinds of factors that have ruined plans in the past, then they move themselves that much closer to maintaining the focus on the needs of the students and schools in the local communities.

Although many who contribute vast sums of money toward education initiatives do so because they have a political agenda, it would not be fair to assume that such philanthropists do not possess the same zeal for improving education as those who may not have tons of financial resources to contribute. Others develop school prototypes that reflect personal ideas about how schools should be designed or what students should be taught. The needs of public schools and students are so vast and complex across communities nationwide that we do not necessarily have the luxury of choosing whom we would prefer as benefactors in education. Further, public education needs a range of initiatives so that prospective entities can pick and choose what might work best in their respective locales. Experience has already proven that programs being funded by wealthy entrepreneurs do make differences in the educational experiences of targeted students. Also, we know that the success of new school models has caused large-scale changes in some school systems. The difficulty with many of these programs is that, sometimes, only a fraction of students in a school or community may benefit, or the programs being implemented are considered less than optimal. Reform is occurring in varying degrees in many places, and none of the initiatives can realistically address the gamut of weaknesses that currently plague local schools. Although many models reflect political or personal agendas, most of them do in fact respond to specific education challenges.

Many attempts at collaboration fail because organizations have not been able to strike the necessary balance of interests or compromise to move forward. Intransigence among partners or the inability to merge organizational goals for enhancing education almost always leads to a dissolution of a partnership. For example, there have been numerous cases wherein school management companies have sought to partner with local schools to operate certain aspects or the whole of school operations. For a variety of reasons—namely, the inability to reach a compromise—many of the proposals never saw the light of day. Without committing to openness, fairness, and equity throughout a collaborative venture, organizations will discover that it will be difficult to trust each other and work together. Most education ventures involve partners who espouse similar ideas about merging their unique assets and expertise in ways that eventually benefit students and schools in their areas. Careful selection and planning in the early stages help mitigate the potential for surprise roadblocks during execution.

A benefactor's inability to fulfill a financial pledge is a reality that partners should weigh carefully as they develop a plan for funding an initiative. Factors that impair an organization's capacity to fund charitable activities are often minimized because funding is usually drawn from liquid assets. Most organizations would not be able to overcome the public embarrassment associated with not being able to make good on a charitable promise, so financial support should be virtually guaranteed if an organization agrees to participate. However, unpredictable outcomes such as economic downturns and personal tragedies can end a program unless alternative funding sources are identified. Notwithstanding that most collaborators probably do not have the luxury of financial backers waiting in line to donate large sums of money, it is definitely a good idea to have a financial contingency plan in place, even if it means scaling back the original blueprint. A contingency plan can also include bringing on new partners to fill the financial gap, either through financial or in-kind contributions.

A loss of strategic focus can lead to all kinds of headaches, interruptions, and problems during the planning and implementation phases. Many partnerships have been destroyed because participating firms have forgotten who their constituents are or what their primary goals are. Even further, some entities get so distracted by external critics and unanticipated outcomes that they begin to engage in activities that are not part of the overall plans. Because school reform is so important and so many groups have such strong opinions about how reform should take place, the level of scrutiny can appear suffocating for some. For those who may be caught off guard by the level of resistance or criticism to their plans in surrounding communities, a strong sense of commitment and focus will have to be exercised; otherwise, they will fall prey to the opposition and cave in to those who support the status quo. The impact of internal and external challenges that may surface during project delivery cannot be measured; however, partnering organizations can take steps to ensure that these factors are properly accounted for and dealt with along the way.

Identifying collaborators who possess the necessary skills and assets to engineer a venture can make or break a proposal. Individual and organizational commitment to a cause is also essential at the start, especially if a collaborative expects to ever get off the ground. There are two schools of thought pertaining to what an optimal number of collaborators would be for any venture. Some believe that the more partners you include, the less likely a few will be saddled with the bulk of costs and responsibilities. Others believe that too many participants lead to competing agendas and ultimately hamper progress. The scope and size of a project have a lot to do with the quality and quantity of entities needed to make a partnership effective. Within the CSC framework, the respective expertise and resources of likely partners vis-à-vis the needs of the targeted schools dictate to a large degree the kinds of entities that should be involved. Without a broad array of participants, CSC cannot reflect the diversity of voices and ideas that can lead to meaningful changes for more students. Although too many collaborators can impede progress and cause a venture to eventually fail, CSC is designed to encourage large numbers of participants to expand the larger debate surrounding public education.

IMPACT OF STAKEHOLDER GROUPS

The state of public education affects many constituency groups within and outside of the education industry. The development and implementation of school reform initiatives are having immediate effects on the daily activities, decisions, and operations of students, parents, classroom teachers, school administrators, and public policymakers. Because so many of the existing weaknesses and inadequacies of local school teaching and learning programs are being ascribed to many of these stakeholders, they are witnessing substantial changes to how they fulfill their daily responsibilities. Proposals that affect the everyday realities for students, teaching professionals, and school administrators are rampant and often far reaching. As a result, these constituencies are justifiably staking their claims and protecting their domains in the constantly evolving school reform debates. Professionals and organizations throughout the nonprofit, private, public, and religious sectors reflect the wider group of stakeholders whose interests are to make sure that education professionals and policymakers are fulfilling their responsibilities and to assist them by developing their own school programs and models. Although the common thread across these sectors and groups pertains to restoring high academic standards for students nationwide, their agendas highlight the varied aspects of the overall education debate.

Many students and parents have been forced to move beyond a habitual sense of comfort about their expectations of school-age education toward a posture of unusually active participation surrounding their choices of elementary and secondary schools. As many local schools have been labeled low performing or inadequate, families are being introduced to education alternatives that reflect academic and extracurricular components that are appealing to young people. Students and parents deserve local schools that will fulfill their mandates to educate at the highest levels. The fact that so many local school systems are not providing workable options or displaying any real propensity toward substantive improvements continues to force families to opt out of neighborhood schools and, in some cases, public schools altogether. The active involvement of so many more parents in shaping the 21st-century education landscape will prove to be significant for a number of reasons. For many years, educators and others criticized parents for not taking an active part in their children's education. Now, we are observing a reversal of that trend. Also, for teaching professionals to be fully effective in their jobs, they continue to need parents to follow through with students and assist them during the time that their children are away from the classroom. The lack of coordination between school and home that exists for so many young people has to disappear so that they can achieve more meaningful academic results. Because the demands on students require much more effort beyond the typical school day, active parental involvement or adult supervision during after-school hours continues to be critical for academic success.

The challenge for local collaborators as they devise plans for school improvement is how to integrate parental involvement in the context of the competing demands on the lives of many parents. As many firms and institutions continue to develop flexible work schedules and work arrangements for their employees, it becomes more practicable for parents to embrace their roles in improving the academic performance of their children. The participation of families in ongoing discussions about raising academic standards for students and schools is integral to the success of an education collaborative. Our efforts to transform how we educate school-age children can be made so much easier by collaborating with parents and other adults who participate in the lives of young people—which is to say, parents and others who supervise youth can facilitate the need to achieve greater coordination between what goes on at school and away from school because of their influence on how these hours are spent. Students, their parents, and adults who play significant roles in students' lives are crucial stakeholders in the push to realize improved academic performance. How we manage their participation in reform initiatives, as well as their willingness to be participants, will affect the outcomes for many students.

Classroom teachers are no longer merely instructors but are largely considered managers of both the academic and the nonacademic activities in the classroom. Coordinating student lesson plans with extracurricular interests while developing other effective learning formats would be a formidable task in any setting. The increased multiplicity of teacher responsibilities is indicative of not only student diversity but also the breadth of challenges confronting students daily. Classroom teachers are spending enormous amounts of time preparing students to succeed on revamped standardized tests that have been recently instituted. As they focus more on achieving standards and benchmarks, teachers are becoming less inclined to develop ancillary learning programs that may actually enhance students' overall academic performance. A separate reality is the increasing pressures being placed on teachers to manage the social, behavioral, and emotional tendencies of school-age children. Although these broadened responsibilities have proven difficult to manage for many in the profession, they also bear witness to the changing roles and expectations throughout the teaching profession.

As we impose higher standards and implement new systems of accountability, we need to do a better job of balancing these requirements with inherent education priorities to create the most effective teaching and learning environments for teachers and students. We cannot compromise the goals of high-quality education by focusing too much on standards and tests. As collaborators in education, we must rely heavily on the knowledge and expertise of classroom instructors because they have the greatest proximity to the students and understand better than anyone what their unique interests and needs are. By partnering with classroom teachers, persons and organizations from other industries and sectors can improve their understanding of the intricacies related to academic and nonacademic activities, which should subsequently enhance their ability to introduce workable solutions for school improvement. The increased standards and new methods of accountability carry great potential for improving student and school academic performance, but they also place a great burden on those who manage the daily teaching and learning activities in the classroom. By combining the skills, resources, and expertise of teachers with those of professionals outside of the education industry, we can help school-age youth achieve prevailing academic standards. The key to the whole quagmire is collaborating effectively with the students, their parents, and school administrators toward the development of programs and activities that are crucial to the overall teaching and learning processes.

As administrators and policymakers establish the requisite standards and guidelines that will propel our students and schools toward higher academic achievement, an important step is to forge workable partnerships with teaching professionals and other stakeholders who possess relevant ideas and expertise. Integrating the perspectives and ideas of classroom teachers into policymaking decisions continues to be an effective means of ensuring that innovations in the classroom make sense from a practical standpoint. Also, the process of incorporating new standards into practice is often made smoother at the micro- or school level because so many administrators and policymakers have spent years teaching in the classroom themselves. However, despite these officials' familiarity with many issues at the local level, merging the disparities between policy requirements and local school capacity continues to be a major challenge. As new standards are implemented, local school officials are often hampered because of a lack of tools and resources to fulfill mandates. The utilization of ideas and experiences from institutional and organizational partners beyond the education arena can help mitigate some of the disparities that are impeding academic progress. Bridging the information and funding gaps between the macro- and micro-levels is an extremely critical step toward realizing substantial improvements in academic achievement.

There are enormous gains to be made if policymakers and school administrators are willing to collaborate with professionals representing other industries and sectors. Many of these persons lead and manage organizations and stakeholders that are similar or more vast in size and diversity to those throughout public school systems. Implementing change and managing disparate stakeholder interests is the same without regard to industry or profession. Overseers of public school systems can extract a lot from the experiences of industries and professions that routinely operate within contexts that constantly change and require real-time adjustments. The macroanalysis and review being applied to public school systems and processes can be addressed in ways that are comparable to the applications in many sectors of private industry. For example, new internal control and reporting requirements being imposed on publicly traded companies can serve as a model for recent school reform policies. Although many companies have complained about the increased costs associated with meeting new industry standards related to increased internal controls and financial reporting, most are taking the steps necessary to respond to the heightened oversight and scrutiny. Public educators can look to these kinds of private-industry experiences to assist them in responding to the higher academic standards that are being implemented at the local school level. Despite their inability to rely on the kinds of alternative funding that is available to many in private industry, public schools may discover new efficiencies and budgetary solutions by collaborating with nontraditional professions and industries. The additional costs pertaining to improved systems of accountability and higher academic standards do not necessarily have to represent a tremendous burden. Through creative partnerships, administrators and teaching professionals can fulfill their mandates in ways that may lead to efficiencies that were previously unimaginable in public education.

LOGISTICAL AND STRUCTURAL CHALLENGES

Although the consensus is that most public schools require immediate and substantive improvements to make them effective once again, the reality is that the path to such a place of efficacy cannot occur without responding to the range of operational, organizational, and structural challenges that will undoubtedly surface. The reengineering of local school operations will inevitably lead to logistical and structural complexities that may seem intractable if not properly assessed and carefully implemented. In this regard, collaborators who develop their proposals in ways that address logistical concerns will be in a better position to partner with constituencies who are familiar with the difficulties of existing school systems and processes. An important element in managing the logistics and structural changes of a new initiative will be securing the support of administrators, parents, teachers, and communities. As each group of constituents seeks assurance that their respective priorities are addressed going forward, a natural quid pro quo will emerge and ideally serve as a tool for negotiation and success. Comprehensive change within public school systems will need to be handled sensibly and strategically by those persons and institutions involved. Strategic coordination and effective communication can ensure that plans and programs make sense in relation to the needs and concerns of those critically important to the ongoing delivery and success of public schools.

Securing the support of key constituency groups is integral to the eventual success of a local school venture. As evidenced by the number of well-intentioned education initiatives that have fallen apart over the past decade, communities, parents, and educators must be recognized as essential voices in public education. These groups possess indispensable knowledge about and experience with the logistics and structures within school systems. Private companies that have attempted to improve or manage individual schools or school districts have failed in part because they did not acknowledge how important certain stakeholders are to the success of a school. No attempt at CSC in elementary and secondary education can succeed without bringing seasoned educators on board. Their expertise in areas such as learning stages, curriculum development, special-needs learning, and student evaluation is invaluable in the development of the structural and logistical aspects of school operations. Because professionals representing the nonprofit, private, and religious sectors are not trained as educators and may not be intimately familiar with different aspects of school operations, the rise and fall of a venture can depend on whether parents, teachers, administrators, and communities choose to sign on as advocates.

Effective management and planning throughout the development and implementation phases can be useful for ensuring that an original blueprint for school reform is not diluted. Furthermore, by carefully coordinating the implementation of an initiative, partners become strategically positioned to anticipate logistical problems along the way. The utilization of a gradual and measured approach can help to ensure that firms and persons do not make hasty decisions that may not account for the most essential components of a venture. Innovations have failed because those leading the way are routinely enticed by a need to answer critics as quickly as possible instead of taking the time necessary to ensure that details are addressed sufficiently. As a result of a rush to completion, important steps can be compromised or ignored, eventually jeopardizing the end product. For example, some education reformers are less inclined to push deadlines back because they fear opponents might view any delay as a weakness or failure. Instead, they proceed as planned and ultimately do not accomplish the intended goals of a proposal. Many scenarios in school reform have failed—some because of a sprint to be the first to implement change and others because of poor management and coordination across participants. The external pressures to succeed in any effort toward local school improvements are real but should not be allowed as incentives that would lead entities to compromise the original vision and plans.

By coordinating plans, actions, and timetables with the overall goals, strategies, and primary interests of critical stakeholders, collaborators can actually minimize the impact of potential logistical and structural complexities. The dedication of resources and expertise by all members within a collaboration, coupled with their careful and strategic planning, can assist in the identification of foreseeable challenges at different stages of implementation. The mere exchange of information, ideas, and experiences during planning and implementation facilitates the timeliness with which problems can be dealt, thereby avoiding major logistical catastrophes. Even still, by establishing mechanisms for problem resolution or crisis management at the outset, collaborators can better manage hurdles along the way. For example, by identifying alternative sources for critical goods and services, participants can minimize the possibilities for delays in service provision or productivity. Similarly, the development of implementation schedules that are not too aggressive but have sufficient lead and idle times built in should help to ensure that projects stay on schedule. Generally, strategic coordination and effective communication among those involved in an education collaborative can lessen the degree to which implementation is stalemated.

Logistical issues may be as simple as figuring out how to integrate external personnel into the daily school routine or as complex as developing transportation schedules to accommodate a new districtwide school-sharing program. Regardless of the circumstances, as communities strategize about the kinds of initiatives that are most relevant to the needs of students in their local schools, assessments have to be made related to the integration of substantive change in the context of restrictions on resources, space, and time. Although some schools can accommodate only limited change, most others are in the enviable position of being able to adapt physical assets, personnel, or academic programs and services in ways that can accommodate teaching and learning innovations. The shifting of personnel between academic programs, the reconfiguration of physical space, and the relocation of school services can require substantial planning, effort, and monitoring to ensure successful transitions. By soliciting the expertise and knowledge of professionals who routinely deal with organizational change in their respective sectors, traditional educators will achieve the advantages inherent in collaboration.

ORGANIZATIONAL CHALLENGES AND OPPORTUNITIES

CSC assumes that participating organizations will work toward fulfilling the goals of an education collaborative within the context of their respective organizational priorities. A successful combination of company-specific goals and the interests of a collaborative can lead to tangible and intangible benefits—for example, schools can begin to see academic improvements, whereas partnering firms can enhance their stature in local communities. Striking a workable balance between the priorities of internal stakeholders and those of external school constituency groups is perhaps the key ingredient to success for most organizations choosing to engage in CSC. This merging of uniquely defined entities around a public issue such as education can be achieved without allowing obstacles such as organizational constraints, hidden agendas, egos, and poor planning to derail the plan. Although it would be unreasonable to assume that these usual impediments to collaboration will not surface, the hope is that the partners' desire to transform their community schools will outweigh the effects of such traditional barriers to collaboration. The presence of strong leadership can help manage the kinds of challenges that typically hamper organizational partnerships.

Perhaps a more daunting task for individual collaborators is how to effectively spread a finite amount of resources across a seemingly infinite number of worthy philanthropic causes. Organizations that establish strategic priorities know precisely what and how much they will dedicate toward charitable activities across several fiscal years. Another advantage for entities that regularly engage in strategic planning is that they clearly know which areas of philanthropy make the most strategic sense (e.g., education, the arts, health care). Although many private and nonprofit enterprises must pay close attention to where they place charitable resources, religious organizations often expand their outreach across a broader range of issues. Developing strategic focus around organizational philanthropy helps to maintain consistency as it relates to the messages being communicated to internal and external stakeholders. Firms and individuals who contribute to charitable activities do so with goals in mind about what they expect to gain from their participation.

It is important for organizations to recognize that their involvement in CSC is not restricted to monetary contributions. In-kind and pro bono donations and services are definite solutions to any number of operational and classroom dilemmas in public schools. Prospective collaborators must be creative and flexible in determining how local schools can benefit from not only the breadth of their expertise but the different kinds of resources at their disposal. The task is not to limit organizational participation to traditional approaches to school improvements but to encourage entities to dialogue about new solutions to the academic challenges confronting students and schools in their communities. To date, large-scale school reform progress may have been hindered by a lack of understanding about the unique and varied roles that different professions and industries can play in elevating public schools. Some of the intransigence in our schools can undoubtedly be resolved by adapting more of the skills and resources of nontraditional partners to the classroom. The charge for CSC participants is to define their unique and specific roles in the contexts of what each entity does well and how that expertise can be translated to address educational needs.

Organizational missions are essentially strategic guides that assist leaders in determining the character of a firm's philanthropic efforts. Because mission statements communicate to internal and external constituencies the primary goals and objectives of an enterprise, leaders must make sure that they allocate and distribute organizational resources in ways that are consistent with the broader mission of the enterprise. Tying charitable activities to a company's strategic vision not only achieves organizational consistency but also ensures that its extracurricular interests maintain the strategic coherence already in place throughout an organization. A critical decision for prospective collaborators is to make sure that their participation complements the existing work of an organization and adds some value, financial or otherwise, to the entity. When choosing to participate in CSC, persons and organizations attempt to enhance their social profile or financial returns through the guise of their charitable activities. Additionally, many consider partnering only with entities that espouse similar values. There are numerous incentives for choosing to collaborate; however, these motivations must be explored in the context of organizational consistency and strategic coherence.

As professionals, sectors, and industries engage in all kinds of partnerships, they will be presented with opportunities to not only enhance their market presence but achieve synergies and efficiencies through cross-subsidization as well as cross-utilization of internal resources. For companies operating in multiple regions, they may determine that the best strategy is to participate in a combination of charitable programs extending across several markets. This would enable them to have a philanthropic presence in a number of their operating markets. Conversely, a smaller local firm might confine its philanthropy to a targeted area to attain greater reach for limited resources. CSC ventures represent real opportunities to broaden the scope and exposure of an organization's products and services. Collaborative efforts built around issues such as public school reform can enhance the public's perception of a firm and its values. There is significant value attached to an organization's participation in programs that are designed to enhance schools. Communities have traditionally exhibited a willingness to patronize and support entities that care about education. Firms and persons should feel good about the level of reciprocity that might be achieved via education partnerships.

As people and organizations dialogue about whether and to what extent to collaborate, the usual concerns related to delegation of duties and responsibilities, levels of investment, and the optimal number of partners will surely surface. Similarly, the size and stature of some entities and the deep pockets of others are realities that can cause some firms to appear superior or inferior. It will be incumbent on the prospective partners to develop a sense of trust with each other to be effective as a partnership. Inevitably though, certain partners will impose their will or vision onto an initiative, which is not necessarily a bad thing when considering that some entity must take a leadership role. The difficulty in this case might relate to multiple entities vying for the role as spokesperson for a collaborative. These kinds of personnel and leadership issues will likely be addressed during the early stages of development and planning. CSC presumes that firms and individuals who choose to work together toward a common good such as improving local schools will strive to ensure that the usual complications associated with partnerships are kept at a minimum.

POLITICAL AND CULTURAL REALITIES

The political and cultural contexts within which school reform initiatives are implemented are as varied as the views about the root causes of the inadequacies and weaknesses in public schools. Some contend that the prevalence of so many poorly qualified teaching professionals and low academic standards are the core issues confronting educators, whereas others believe that insufficient resources and deficient systems and structures represent the essence of the challenges facing public school systems. Although both schools of thought are on point, each can be attributed to a common refrain being heard from mainstream conservative and liberal politicos. As prospective collaborators examine the uniqueness of schools in their neighborhoods and communities, their focus has to be directed more toward the needs of their target audiences and less on which political stance is more likely to be agreeable with their planned initiatives. Collaborators will likely have to exhibit a healthy dose of political correctness to appease stakeholder groups that are often as diverse as their respective political views and agendas.

School changes that are initiated by persons or organizations outside of the traditional education arena are sometimes manifestations of individual or corporate politics. These same politics can translate into platforms that lead to student improvements in critical academic areas or even test scores. Whether coincidental or intended, collaborators can definitely take advantage of preexisting political motives by piggybacking on individual or corporate interventions in education. However, from an overall standpoint, they should take steps to ensure that the academic priorities of targeted communities are appropriately matched with the eventual blueprint. The coupling of clear and concise academic strategies and goals with specific means of attaining the objectives can ensure that proposals maintain a high degree of relevance in relation to the dilemmas facing local schools. It is worth noting that the mere existence of a politically motivated agenda can inadvertently deter an initiative away from its intended purpose, unless participants are paying close attention throughout the planning and development phases. Clarity of purpose and persistence can serve any group of collaborators well, especially in the context of ancillary motives that may be colored by politics.

Political motivations are merely one of numerous reasons that so many persons and organizations are engaging in the school reform movement. Other entities from the nonprofit, private, and religious sectors participate because of a personal commitment, a sense of social responsibility, corporate campaigns, or just simply personal experiences. Whatever the rationale, each is a legitimate incentive and offers meaningful insight for selecting partners and working effectively with them once they get on board. Firms and individuals who are committed to school reform can be viewed as being more insistent on following a venture through to the end and not abandoning it midway through the process. In other words, those whose involvement can be tied to a sense of responsibility or investment are perhaps more likely to shepherd the proposal to fruition. Conversely, because of varying factors (e.g., annual budget changes, personnel changes), those who participate by way of corporate campaigns may not be around for the duration. Whatever the scenario, it is important to know a partner's underlying motivation and the level of intended commitment. A healthy mixture of short- and long-term partners can help promote consistency and stability, especially given that most reform efforts extend across many years.

Contemporary political realities will inevitably play a significant role in the character and structure of elementary and secondary schools primarily because the policies and guidelines governing public school systems are established and implemented within the political arena. CSC participants must not shy away from political forces in their communities as they pertain to education. They must be willing to engage an array of opinions about how best to improve schools while examining the political, economic, and social dimensions of reform proposals. Collaborators may find themselves in the precarious position of trying to maintain their independence or neutrality from a group or political persuasion while simultaneously accommodating the priorities of key constituencies. Maintaining a posture of diversity and impartiality are important elements that can lead to broader acceptance. CSC encourages diverse perspectives and organizations to collaborate in ways that can ultimately integrate differing political perspectives. It would be nice to see individuals and institutions across the political spectrum working together, creating innovative solutions in public education without regard to political concerns or agendas.

Indeed, there will be many who will have defined their own forms of intervention and will care very little about attempts to collaborate. Those who advocate certain political points of view may only be interested in partnering with entities that share their established ideas and beliefs about the nature of the problems in public schools. For example, organizations that have concluded that academic standards need to be raised to elevate schools may not want to discuss with other firms the possibility of upgrading or reengineering school systems and learning processes before increasing the standards. Likewise, firms that subscribe to a more comprehensive approach to reform will most likely appeal to prospective partners who are concerned with fixing some of the broken processes and systems within local schools. The politics of influence and stature will play a significant role in many communities whereby those who possess substantial resources and credible networks will find themselves in the stronger position of being able to dictate the character of a venture by virtue of their clout and access to resources.

The established culture and politics of local school systems will affect the ability of nontraditional partners to enter the education arena. Many failed attempts by private entrepreneurs and companies to manage or privatize schools can be attributed to either their lack of understanding of acceptable mores and traditions pertaining to respective schools or their inability to collaborate with key constituencies within local communities. Historically, the oversight or stewardship of public schools has tended toward a territorial and insular existence, which has translated into skepticism toward new entrants into established territory. Many school leaders and constituents have created such intransigence throughout school districts that the only real opportunity for change has to come from beyond the establishment because everyone within the bureaucracy pretty much marches to one beat. These realities underscore the importance of collaborating with firms and persons who already possess significant local area knowledge and history pertaining to local school leadership and administration. In situations where local school politics elicits great passion from certain constituencies, it will be extremely critical to have influential and resourceful community partners on one's side. Under these kinds of circumstances, it will not be a useful or productive endeavor if CSC partners are not able to develop effective means of engaging local stakeholders in the process.

The political sensibilities of neighborhoods and communities can be gauged more effectively when a partnership consists of entities that have a longtime history in an area or possess great knowledge about the community. A community's perception about organizational participation in local school reform can be influenced by who is leading the change. Familiar names and faces always carry more clout and credence when the topic of discussion is changing something that has existed in a certain form for generations. Knowing the particular interests and priorities of community groups as they pertain to schools can help to shape the eventual landscape for public schools. Regardless of political or cultural differences, collaboration among entities representing the entire spectrum of ideas and perspectives can be accomplished primarily because so many are personally committed and feel a sense of social and professional responsibility to improving education.

The crisis state of local schools all over the country calls for unusual levels of commitment and persistence by persons and organizations that may not have been considered likely partners. Despite many of the aforementioned challenges and realities that regularly plague attempts at collaboration, the hope is that the huge need to transform elementary and secondary schools nationwide will motivate participants from all sectors to work desperately toward workable solutions. The shared obligation by so many to not only contribute to public school reform but also participate in the academic training of our future leaders and workers can form the essential foundation for large-scale cross-sectoral involvement. Many of the impending challenges to collaboration can be mitigated by including a broad spectrum of organizations from the respective communities as well as by maintaining a sense of purpose and focus from planning to execution. Partnerships that are characterized by strong leadership and adequate sharing of roles and responsibilities stand better chances of collaborative success than do those that may be hampered by hidden agendas or lack of commitment.

5

BEYOND THE WALLS OF THE "CHURCH"

A SECTOR IN TRANSITION

The shifting focus of the faith community beyond its walls has reshaped the ministerial agendas of practically every religious entity as each seeks to maintain relevance in the lives of its parishioners and the surrounding communities. The mere expansion of some ministries into areas such as education and community development has essentially inspired a larger segment of the sector to shift its emphasis as well. Perhaps, the most encouraging aspect of this transition is that communities of faith are providing practical interpretations and applications of their teachings and doctrines for their audiences. People of faith no longer have to wonder how to express their social, economic, and political ideas and positions in the context of their religious beliefs. Their spiritual and religious leaders are developing ministries that enable them to apply their beliefs to everyday issues and concerns.

This redefinition and refinement of ministerial mandates is occurring during a period in history wherein people of all faiths and religions are seeking more guidance and interpretation from their spiritual leaders as they become confronted with complex personal, professional, and public dilemmas. For a larger percentage of the population, religion and spirituality are playing a more significant role in everyday lives. This increasing reality is presenting the religious sector with access to a broader audience, community relevance, and growth potential. This type of institutional status and access to large numbers of people hints at the critical role that the sector can play in CSC. Although religious institutions have always been significant forces in communities, the prevailing realities suggest that, now more than ever, they are influential voices for increasing numbers of people. Their local presence, community influence, community prominence, and the reverence of their leaders can be translated into substantive change for communities seeking leadership and reform in areas such as education.

A separate dimension of the shifting focus beyond the walls of the church is the growth of interfaith collaborations, ecumenical ventures, and church coalitions. Religious leaders operating in communities that are close in proximity and mission are discovering that they have comparable ministerial concerns and are willing to engage one another in devising meaningful programs and initiatives that address specific concerns in their neighborhoods and communities. Clerics representing different denominations and faiths have begun to acknowledge their institutional connectedness as well as the shared dilemmas of their respective constituents. The sector's capacity to collaboratively respond to issues is allowing it to speak with a louder voice and have an even greater impact on targeted issues. Partnerships among religious organizations can play significant roles in addressing problems such as inadequate schools. The influence of these institutions can lead to broad exposure and, sometimes, more rapid responses to social or public concerns that may otherwise get caught up in bureaucracy or politics.

One example of how communities of faith are collaborating to address public issues is the Boston TenPoint Coalition, an ecumenical group of Christian clergy and lay leaders based in Boston. This coalition builds partnerships with institutions from all sectors whose interests include the revitalization of families and communities, with specific emphasis on serving high-risk youth. The group's work with local schools has been instrumental in redirecting youth behavior and attitudes away from nonproductive activities. A separate approach to collaboration has been employed by the Windsor Village United Methodist Church of Houston in its creation of the Pyramid Community Development Corporation. This nonprofit has partnered with local entities from the public and private sectors to build programs and enterprises that respond to educational, social, economic, spiritual, and medical needs of the church membership and the surrounding community. Pyramid's most prominent partnership effort has been the completion of a multiuse complex that houses a bank, community college, health clinic, and office suites.

For decades, this sector has played an important role in providing access to elementary and secondary education through its parochial schools. Many of these church-based learning facilities are filling gaps created by public schools' inability to properly educate all children equally and fairly. Catholic and other Christian schools in urban communities continue to be a refuge for many families seeking a disciplined environment and comprehensive curriculum for their school-age children. Parochial schools seem to display an inclination toward nurturing students in areas beyond the "hard" academic subjects. A curriculum that emphasizes values, ethics, and morals is important to many parents who are actively involved in their children's education. This sector's ability to educate the whole child speaks largely to its potential involvement and leadership in CSC. Some of what is missing in many public schools is an understanding of the need to address the "soft," nonacademic areas affecting school-age children's development. What parochial schools are successful at is incorporating these aspects into the overall educational plans of their schools. Moral and ethical themes are not commonly viewed as being essential to the academic achievement of young people. Although the emphasis has justifiably and rightfully been placed on hard academic subjects, the incorporation of soft topics into education may move us closer to fulfilling our overall objectives for school-age learning.

An example of a church-based school that blends a religious and secular education by offering a rigorous curriculum alongside Christian values is the Allen Christian School, in Jamaica, New York. Founded in 1982 as a preK–8 school, the school has produced graduates who attend some of the most prestigious high schools in metropolitan New York City. An examination of the course offerings and extracurricular activities of this Christian school reveals a focus on fundamentals such as reading, math, and language arts, as well as instruction in ethics, the arts, technology, and Christian education. Allen's small class sizes foster the high degree of student–teacher interaction that it claims as a trademark of the school.

Similarly, by dividing into "house teams," a family-oriented environment is created that allows faculty to closely understand the unique strengths and weaknesses of individual students.

RELIGIOUS-SECTOR ROLES IN CSC

The religious sector is commonly viewed as that part of society that responds to the spiritual and religious needs of people. The range of religious communities forming this sector includes churches, parishes, synagogues, mosques, temples, and so on. There are also numerous denominations or faiths that compose this sector (e.g., Christianity, Judaism, Islam, Buddhism). Apart from the institutions established primarily to accommodate the worship needs and experiences of the constituents, a new segment of the sector has emerged that consists of nonprofit subsidiaries that respond to a range of social, political, cultural, and economic concerns. The organizations making up this segment not only support the work of the larger institutions but also represent practical interpretations of the spiritual and religious mandates of the leaders and denominations. Although religious institutions have never existed apart from their social, political, economic, and cultural realities, they had not established such large numbers of distinct subsidiaries to respond to these concerns until the latter half of the 20th century. This segment of church nonprofits includes social-justice organizations, community and economic development corporations, political advocacy groups, denominational entities, public-policy agencies, drug and alcohol rehabilitation programs, youth enrichment programs, employment services, financial services, and court advocacy programs. The focuses of these subsidiaries include job creation, housing, senior citizen concerns, health care, financial services, commercial and retail ventures, schools, social justice, human rights, and political advocacy.

The broad range of entities making up the religious sector is primarily a tribute to leadership that has acknowledged not only the critical role of religion and spirituality in people's lives but also the importance of displaying a willingness and commitment to minister to the whole person. The social service and political emphases across the sector have grown tremendously and have been instrumental in how organizations respond to the multitude of needs facing their communities and constituents. This sector is similar to the nonprofit sector in that it seeks to fill voids created by market inefficiencies and other inadequacies of private markets. Also, the sector serves as a type of moral and spiritual barometer for the rest of society as its members work to close economic gaps in the lives of so many whose needs are routinely ignored by mainstream economic and social enterprises. As stewards of those who are often marginalized by society, religious voices can instill a sense of realism and compassion into any collaborative endeavor. Similarly, by remaining committed to the dismantling of social, economic, and cultural barriers, religious institutions can help secular entities recognize that they are sometimes participants in the perpetuation of certain obstacles and barriers for others.

The church as a de facto *moral and ethical barometer* for local communities can be a strong voice in CSC. Just as many parishioners are looking to their spiritual and religious leaders for instruction in the areas of personal ethics and morals, the public at large expects similar guidance from those who have been endowed as de facto stewards of how we conduct ourselves, morally and ethically in contemporary life. Because the generally agreed-on mandate of most religious entities is to serve as a sort of guardian over and interpreter of individual perceptions and beliefs about private and public morals and ethics in the context of religion and spirituality, it makes sense that this sector can serve as a moral guide for organizations working together to improve schools. The objective would be for religious participants to instruct and lead in a manner that can produce high standards of justice and fairness, to be utilized in the development of world-class public schools. Where our religious entities can present for us the theoretical framework for morality, ethics, and values, we can develop a practical road map to get us to a destination marked by an increased emphasis in these areas of human tendencies and conduct.

The hope is that this sector's participants will lead the others in establishing programs and structures that produce equity and access for all children being served. Any attempt to transform schools must be based on the reality that every child has the right to a high-quality education. Further, the delivery of this education must be distributed equitably to ensure equal access and equal resources for communities of all shapes, sizes, and colors. One of the major weaknesses of many school systems is the extreme inequity across schools in terms of the distribution of resources, teacher quality, and facilities readiness. Because the religious community as well as the nonprofit sector works closely with underserved groups in communities, it could use its experiences to lead and inform CSC partners in devising plans for responding to the educational needs of children from a broad spectrum of groups. By helping the partners focus on justice and fairness as important aspects of morality and ethics, the religious sector can guide a partnership toward doing a better job of producing schools that offer all school-age children in a community an equal opportunity for educational success.

The *reverential leadership and influence* commonly associated with leaders of churches, parishes, synagogues, mosques, and temples reflect another aspect of this sector's potential to play a strong role in CSC. Their influence throughout the surrounding communities can be significant as it relates to communicating to the public how a school or affiliate venture would enhance the educational opportunities for youth in a local area. Citizens are more likely to listen to someone whom they respect and trust and who they believe possess their best interests—which is to say, individual and organizational members of a community are more inclined to rally behind a project being spearheaded by someone whom they know as a leader and whose leadership they respect. Similarly, persons and organizations representing the other sectors are more likely to become engaged in a CSC venture that is being convened by a respected or influential leader of a community, someone who can or already has sifted through the nuances and intricacies related to community mores and politics. To create a groundswell of interest and publicity around transforming local area schools, CSC partners will need to rely heavily on the influence and stature of religious and spiritual leaders in an area. If the partners can create enough community interest and involvement in local school reform, then the task is halfway complete. Once they have the citizens' attention, they will find it easier to engage in serious and substantive dialogue around improving schools.

Families and concerned citizens of communities have shown in recent years that they attach a high level of skepticism to any new, innovative, or nontraditional idea pertaining to the reform of local schools. In cases where the reform effort is being initiated by private companies or other nontraditional partners in education, an innate sense of distrust seems to dominate. Recent experiments in local school reform appear to have failed because the citizenry was not perceived as a critical stakeholder group in the early stages of planning and strategizing. Implicit in CSC is the reality that parents and children are primary constituents in any collaboration whose goal is the transformation of schools. This collaborative framework will never succeed without incorporating the priorities of its most critical stakeholder groups (i.e., parents, students, and communities). Just as equity and fairness will be crucial in terms of ensuring how well we serve the youth, we must be adamant about openness and diversity when dialoguing and partnering with parents and local citizens. The expectation at the outset has to be to respect and honor the perspectives of every key stakeholder group; otherwise, we fall prey to the same mistakes made by others who have attempted school reform. An introductory debriefing to the community by members of the religious sector can go a long way toward mitigating many of the fears and anxieties that have been expressed by various citizens groups about innovative, nontraditional approaches to school reform.

The *community prominence and community relevance* of churches, synagogues, mosques, parishes, temples, and so forth, are intangible representations of how critical a role religious organizations will play in CSC. Further, the accessibility and visibility of these institutions in any community are evidence of their importance and status in the minds of the parishioners and the citizens who observe from afar. An important denominator for CSC is the willingness of the citizenry to accept new ideas about improving schools. Without the support and direct involvement of religious organizations that are held in high esteem by local residents, collaborators do not stand a good chance at encouraging the residents to accept their plans. The prominence and relevance of the institutions essentially determine the degree to which this sector's influence can be translated into meaningful support for innovative changes in neighborhood schools.

Places of worship are increasingly identified as focal points in communities, partly because they respond to a range of constituent needs. Many function as conduits for or distributors of a range of social, economic, and community services. The fact that governmental agencies are entrusting faith communities with certain social service responsibilities enhances the accessibility, visibility, relevance, and prominence of religious institutions in their local areas. Because religious organizations often operate as a type of intermediary or mediator between groups within a community, many of these groups seek religious organizations' leadership and guidance when resolving local problems. A separate utility of local churches is that they usually house banquet halls and large meeting facilities that can accommodate large numbers of people for community town hall meetings and other types of gatherings. As a provider of multiple services to its neighbors, houses of worship are strategically positioned to serve as key players in CSC.

In communities where social service agencies are scarce or simply ineffective, the public sector relies heavily on churches or organizations that are affiliated with them to disburse and deliver services such as job placement and training, homeownership seminars, recreational programs, court advocacy, family assistance, dissemination of medical and public health information, senior citizens programs, and child welfare programs. Many religious organizations provide meals and other necessary goods and services to persons who have been temporarily displaced from their homes and unemployed. Federal dollars are often available to support the provision of these services at the local level. It is worth noting again that many religious organizations have established separate entities to accommodate this range of services being delivered via the church. The work of these church-affiliated nonprofit organizations is consistent with that of many other nonprofit entities whose focus is on meeting social and economic needs of targeted groups.

Religious entities that operate effectively in their respective communities do so because local citizens value the dual roles that they play in people's lives, serving both as spiritual guide and provider of social and community services. The increasing role of religion and spirituality in the personal sphere of individual life adds weight to how important this sector's participation can be in CSC. The phenomenal membership growth being experienced by many in the sector signifies even greater opportunities for access to a critical mass in a community. The goal is to build on the access and take advantage of the opportunities that stem from their existent place of prominence in people's personal lives. Individual reliance on spiritual and religious leaders cannot be underestimated in its capacity to influence decisions about education and various other issues that affect daily life.

EXAMPLES OF RELIGIOUS-SECTOR PARTICIPATION IN CSC

To date, religious-sector participation in education has consisted of models such as church-affiliated schools, after-school programs, mentoring programs, literacy initiatives, and tutoring assistance. Through CSC, faith communities can continue these types of programs in collaboration with organizations from different sectors. The form that the participation takes is not as important as the decision and commitment to play a part in the partnership itself. For all of the reasons described throughout this chapter, religious institutions are integral to ensuring the success of CSC projects in local communities. As is the case with most organizations, the temptation to expend too much of scarce resources will need to be adequately balanced against the desire to fulfill an organization's vision as it pertains to education reform. Whether as the convener or one of the partner organizations, religious-sector entities face numerous opportunities to help in improving local schools while fulfilling their ministerial responsibilities to neighboring communities.

An aggressive approach to participation in school reform might consist of a church's securing an actual charter to form a new school. Most publicly funded charter initiatives allow nontraditional professionals and organizations to apply for elementary and secondary school charters. Through a charter initiative, a church can gain access to the same per-pupil expenditures that traditional public schools have. This would undoubtedly mitigate a great deal of the financial investment required for school operations. By attracting partners from the nonprofit and private sectors, additional nonfinancial as well as financial resources may be secured. The ability to encourage cross-sectoral participation in the charter application process can be viewed as enhancing the chances of being awarded an actual charter, depending on which legislative body is making the final decision. Maintaining a strong sense of independence and equity in the implementation of a charter school poses a unique challenge for religious organizations because they are accustomed to their own doctrinal beliefs and may not be too inclined toward utilizing unbiased, neutral programs and curricula. As long as public funding is not used in a manner that preferences some to the exclusion of others, a charter school initiative should be able to avoid some of the intense public scrutiny and opposition that has been the experience of some recent charter holders. Because this type of charter scenario essentially places taxpayer dollars in the hands of a religious entity, maintaining a posture of impartiality and nonsectarianism is of paramount concern.

There are some religious institutions that have been able to start independent schools in collaboration with local private- and public-sector enterprises. Without regard to the religious nature of the school, there are firms that have been willing to share their expertise and resources to contribute to the enhancement of schools in their communities. The strength of the leadership and the actual work of a religious institution in a community are key factors in being able to attract firms from other sectors. Most consider the good deeds and effectiveness of religious organizations as sufficient evidence to warrant their investment in a school. Indeed, the ideal situation for most churches is to be able to form a new school that emulates and incorporates the beliefs and teachings of the respective church ministry. To be able to attract institutional partners from the nonprofit, private, and public sectors without altering any of the school philosophies or policies presents an even more appealing scenario. However, this type of arrangement is probably the exception more than the rule, given the range of competing interests with which an entity has to contend. There are unique circumstances that lend themselves to being able to build a school consistent with the larger vision and mission of a church while securing external partners along the way. An example of this is a partnership between an entrepreneur whose religious beliefs are closely aligned with those of a particular church.

There are numerous other opportunities for religious institutions to engage in some form of collaboration across sectors. A few examples of ancillary programs include after-school social and cultural activities, academic tutoring sessions on Saturday mornings, school-age mentoring programs, dramatic-arts classes, instrumental-music lessons, and summer sports leagues. Because many school districts have eliminated sports, music, arts, and physical education from their budgets, a gap in the creative, athletic, and artistic activities for young people has been the result. Some churches have discovered that there is in fact private and public funding available to assist with the provision of many of these extracurricular activities. Private foundations, companies, and entrepreneurs who want to ensure that young people are exposed to the arts, music, and athletics have targeted funds available to disburse in these areas. Although federal and state funding has decreased for these activities, the public sector continues to seek outside organizations to implement extracurricular programs that were previously within the domain of public schools.

The tremendous growth in physical space being utilized by the growing phenomenon known as "megachurches" can be translated into a real advantage for a CSC project seeking space to house a school. Many of these large churches operate on campuses that occupy many acres and miles of land. The fact that many churches do not use much of their physical space during certain hours of a week makes this option even more appealing. The possibility of leasing church facilities for use as a school is a win-win situation for both sides. In addition to housing an actual school, many of the ancillary educational and extracurricular programs discussed earlier may be operated out of church facilities as well. One of the greatest challenges in forming a school lies in securing and financing the actual physical space. The underutilized physical capacity of many religious institutions can be a significant advantage for the religious concern itself and the CSC collaboration as a whole. Being able to utilize physical assets in a manner that facilitates local school improvements would not only serve the youth of a community but represent a real strategic advantage for the religious sector as it identifies its true distinctive competencies in the context of school reform.

CHURCH–STATE CHALLENGES

Inevitably, many will scrutinize and question whether religious organizations have any business participating in education reform at all. The usual controversy surrounding the use of public funds and services to support parochial schools will undoubtedly rear its ugly head. The perennial questions pertaining to whether parochial schools are entitled to share computers, libraries, equipment, and other instructional materials with public schools will be raised. The use of public funds to subsidize voucher programs that allow students to attend parochial, private, and independent schools will continue to be a hotbed issue for many who are focused on the separation of church and state. Just as the ardent supporters of the church–state separation are intent on protecting the judicial mandate, CSC similarly underscores how important it is for the government to not be viewed as supporting a particular religion; instead, it must play the role as an advocate of religious diversity. Part of the great promise for CSC is its plans to capitalize on the diversity of persons and organizations that compose all of the sectors in local communities. With regard to religious diversity, the goals of CSC are to encourage a broad range of voices from religion to participate in transforming schools.

CSC will not jeopardize the constitutionally mandated distinction between church and state by including the religious sector in its strategic framework. The intent is not to incorporate particular beliefs, doctrines, and principles of a religion into the development of school curricula, plans, and programs. Rather, the expectation is to build on the moral and ethical leadership, community influence, access, and prominence of local religious entities as schools are formed. To the extent that certain religions advocate high standards of morality and ethics, CSC could be found guilty of advocating on behalf of those religions. A prominent feature of this collaborative framework is to ensure that groups and communities are served adequately, equitably, justly, and fairly. The expectation is that religious participants will assist the other organizations and professionals in ensuring that constituents are indeed served properly in these contexts.

As expressed previously, a real challenge for the religious sector in CSC is how to successfully maintain a posture of independence, neutrality, and impartiality throughout the process, without being accused of proselytizing or indoctrination. Although many will continue to misrepresent the actual intent of the sector, especially as it pertains to public schools, it will be incumbent on the partner organizations from the different sectors to ensure that the integrity of the partnership is maintained and not compromised by some sort of underhanded attempt to distort educational value by incorporating the beliefs and philosophies of a particular religion in the school prototype. For those prospective participants who may be interested in the promulgation of religious doctrine in school-age education, they should seek other means for disseminating their messages. As advocates of CSC, we will not allow its integrity to be compromised by institutions seeking to manipulate the broader purposes of the framework with their own hidden agendas. Where particular religious beliefs coincide with the educational ideals that the group establishes, one might observe the practical application of these values.

The concerns about the use of public dollars to support parochial schools via the sharing of goods and services or voucher initiatives are mitigated in several ways. Where a charter is awarded to a religious entity, there is little chance that the church or other community of faith could stack the curriculum in its favor because many of the preestablished guidelines for traditional public schools apply to charter schools. Moreover, to ensure that all students have equal access, enrollment is usually determined by a lottery system. Regarding the use of public funds by churches to operate many of the ancillary programs, the fact that a particular church runs a program has not excluded persons who are not members of a local church from taking part in a program. Because the awarding of the funds is often intended to benefit a whole community, the church merely serves as a facilitator or distributor on behalf of the respective governmental entity.

Although the concerns regarding the nature and intent of religious-sector participation in CSC may be legitimate, we cannot allow them to hinder our efforts to utilize the strengths and access of the sector. It is imperative that we eliminate the traditional tendencies and fears related to working with religious institutions. We cannot allow zealots and ideologues to prevent us from engaging in constructive dialogue and actions that may lead toward a brighter future for our children. Indeed, we must ensure that we do not violate the constitutionality of the separation of church and state. The expectation is that the individual and institutional partners will apply sufficient oversight and wisdom in their efforts to produce models that are marked by integrity and impartiality. There are numerous contemporary examples of how to effectively maneuver within the judicial and legal constraints of church–state parameters, without compromising the spirit of the mandate. By learning from some of these experiences and moving beyond our fears, we can capitalize on the assets and expertise within the religious sector. Last, as we strategize about the appropriate ways for the faith community to provide service in local areas, perhaps we can draw inspiration and guidance from Daniel L. Migliore's *Faith Seeking Understanding* in his warning to the church:

> If the church as herald is not to be an instrument of domination, it must be willing to be instructed by others how it might best be of service to them and, equally important, what they may have to give as well as receive. Moreover, a holistic understanding of service is often missing from this model. Preoccupation with the delivery of the message may override the concern to meet concrete human needs for food, shelter, medical care, education, and other basics of dignified human life. (p. 196)

REFERENCE

Migliore, D. L. (2004). *Faith seeking understanding: An introduction to Christian theology* (2nd ed.). Grand Rapids, MI: Eerdmans.

6

THE PROMINENCE OF THE NONPROFIT COMMUNITY

GROWTH IN THE PRESENCE AND WORK OF NONPROFITS

The nonprofit sector largely comprises entities that hold a status as tax-exempt organizations and whose focuses tend to be social service. Included in this group are social service agencies, colleges and universities, artistic and cultural organizations, foundations, community development financial institutions, political action committees, think tanks, civic groups, and trade associations. Depending on stakeholder interests and the nature of the work, many nonprofit firms can be categorized as private- or public-sector firms. The social service focus of many of these organizations establishes what is unique about them. Their commitment to relevant issues in their surrounding neighborhoods and communities enables them to more effectively respond to localized needs. Likewise, their presence in the communities and accumulated local knowledge establish their credibility in the eyes of the constituents.

A separate characteristic of many nonprofits is that they are often more effective at smaller-scale initiatives than are some of the larger private firms that may not know a particular region. This sector's emphasis on specific groups and their respective priorities reflects the essence of what is distinctive about organizations that focus largely on social and public concerns. By addressing specific isolated issues, nonprofits place themselves at a strategic advantage over other types of enterprises. The inability of public- and private-sector entities to create effective solutions to some local problems has essentially created a niche advantage for the nonprofit community. Because many private and public entities are so large and operate in so many disparate markets, they are often not able to properly address the demands and priorities of a targeted market. The distinctive competencies of the sector (i.e., local presence and localized knowledge and focus) underscore how important this kind of enterprise can be for local regions and communities.

The willingness to provide economic and social options in markets that are poorly served or not served at all distinguishes the nonprofit community from others. By responding to issues and groups whose needs remain unfulfilled by traditional private market solutions, nonprofits focus the attention of other sectors toward groups that warrant specialized or nonconventional resources and services. Nonprofits commonly address market needs by offering creative solutions that allow members of isolated communities to enjoy benefits similar to those available in the mainstream marketplace. As a result of nonprofit interventions, groups that tend to be underserved gain opportunities and advantages that mirror those throughout the larger economy. Their proximity to constituents, established relationships, and networks within communities are significant factors in determining their degree of success in a local area. As an example, their knowledge about underserved and unserved groups in an area can prove to be invaluable in a collaborative venture with a multinational corporation seeking to become involved in school reform in a particular region.

Over the past few decades, there has been a tremendous shift in the kinds of work being performed by nonprofit-sector enterprises. Ranging from large multiaffiliate organizations such as the United Way, the National Urban League, Boys and Girls Clubs of America, and the Red Cross to stand-alone local service providers, the entire spectrum of nonprofit work and service has expanded. The prominence of this sector has been elevated, along with the growing recognition that its member organizations have the capacity to provide a range of services that other firms have found elusive. The sector's members are consistently gravitating toward the production and distribution of goods and services that have traditionally been the domain of private enterprise. The financing of single and multifamily homes, the creation of jobs, and the provision of financial management by nonprofits cause them to sometimes look like quasi-private enterprises. As they have expanded their overall missions to include addressing the full range of needs of their constituents, they have begun to consider ways of responding to the educational needs of youth. The sector is basically playing a complementary role as it piggybacks on the work of other sectors but does so with more specificity. This type of work and role sharing occurring in the marketplace bodes well for the success of CSC.

Nonprofits continue to be essential to the broader public as they relate to the need to understand characteristics and patterns of select groups within a community. Their history of maintaining a sense of the events and trends within neighborhoods has been invaluable on many fronts. Politicians as well as businesspeople understand the important position held by local entities because more than likely they can interpret and place the events of a community in their proper contexts. To maintain effective service records, nonprofits are constantly translating the intricacies and nuances that are unique to ethnic and demographic groups residing in their locales. Recognition of the traditions, mores, and other demographic factors of the respective groups makes this sector's work much more relevant. Similar to their religious counterparts, nonprofit institutions are central in the lives of many citizens who may not be adequately served by mainstream goods and services providers. This sector's willingness to create solutions that are customized for specific markets highlights the importance of its work and establishes its eminence in our society.

The community prominence and influence of nonprofits are derived from their capacity to respond to the everyday needs. The service profiles and histories of these local enterprises are key indicators of their potential to add value to the lives of the people. Local citizens can readily point to programs and services that are being made available to them through the work of their local nonprofits. The provision of affordable housing, clothing, food, employment assistance, and comprehensive medical services are some ways by which nonprofits have matched their organizational capacities with local area priorities. By responding to these types of immediate needs, nonprofits do effectively fill economic and social gaps in people's lives. This also ensures that the organizations remain visible and prominent in the minds of the people. Religious- and nonprofit-sector organizations remain vital institutions in their communities because they are increasingly able to address those needs that are deemed important and central to constituents' livelihood. The local influence of these institutions is consistently substantiated by their track records and their capacities to respond to citizens' priorities.

Historically, many enterprises within the sector have arisen because someone believed that there was a need or gap in services being offered to local citizenry. Just as the mission of an entity drives which segments are targeted, the vested interests of the entity's stakeholders often dictate the identification of these segments. The actual support of board members, officers, and benefactors is quite often linked to the creation of area programming. This sector's willingness to specify programs and funding for groups that possess greater needs has successfully filled gaps in a variety of ways. For example, private foundations' financial support of postsecondary educational research fellowships in traditionally neglected areas and for targeted students has been the difference in many instances. Separately, a microenterprise entity that offers loans and grants to local entrepreneurs has contributed to the overall sustainability of some communities. Although many private-, religious-, and public-sector entities may be constrained by their self-imposed policies and guidelines, nonprofits may have flexibility with the type of intervention and assistance that they can offer.

The work of nonprofits continues to be primarily concentrated in the areas of social service and economic development at the local or state levels, although there are identifiable nonprofits whose work is primarily focused on global concerns. The sector's expansion into areas such as investments, education, job creation, and public health reflects the broadened missions of the member organizations. These expanded portfolios are indicative of the sector's flexibility and breadth in terms of its programming. As nonprofits continue to expand their work to embrace the building of productive, sustainable local neighborhoods and communities, their roles and the expectations of them in the larger society will continue to broaden. Their experience in complementing and collaborating with other sectors to fill the economic and social gaps that result from market inefficiencies and other sectoral inadequacies portends their indispensable role in CSC. By participating in the transformation of nonperforming schools, this sector's institutions will continue to discover that their work is consistent with their broader objectives for targeted communities. Not many could have predicted decades ago that nonprofits would play such a vital role in the transformation of so many neighborhoods and communities. The phenomenal expansion that has occurred in the sector is a tribute to the commitment of the organizations and their willingness to extend their missions beyond traditional and sectoral boundaries.

The National Urban League, a national nonprofit that oversees more than 100 local affiliates across many states, has traditionally been known for work in communities that is designed to assist African Americans in securing economic and social parity. An important component of its mission has been the provision of educational programs that offer youth the best opportunities for a high-quality education. The league's national and local offices have partnered with foundations, corporations, and governmental agencies to provide after-school programs, corporate mentoring programs, online book clubs, literacy initiatives, and college scholarships. All of these programs are intended to instill a sense of pride and attainability in the minds of youth vis-à-vis the prevailing youth culture. The mission of the league is to ensure that young people understand that the achievement of economic and social equity is inextricably linked to obtaining a quality education.

The Local Initiatives Support Corporation (LISC) works directly with corporations, governmental agencies, philanthropic interests, and other local nonprofits in their shared missions to transform distressed communities into healthy, sustainable ones; the creation of public schools that work and deliver quality public education is a critical component of this mission. To help bridge the educational facilities' financing gap, LISC houses the Educational Facilities Financing Center, which has provided over $30 million in grants, loans, and loan guarantees to public charter schools. Through its network of more than 30 local offices, this national nonprofit has successfully pooled the resources of public and private funding entities to create funds totaling over $50 million to finance the renovation or construction of charter school facilities. LISC has awarded the Knowledge Is Power Program a $1 million loan to help build and renovate facilities.

NONPROFIT ROLES IN CSC

One fundamental difference between nonprofits and many other organizations is their role as a type of *local service barometer*. Their ability to interpret market opportunities and then create concrete solutions for these markets confirms how crucial they can be for local market intervention. Nonprofits' history of providing communities with tailored products and services not only validates the unique contributions that they can bring to a collaborative effort but also accentuates the leadership of nonprofit enterprise in local community life. Their legacy of community intervention and service can be instructive for the other sectors as they collaborate around education reform. The *proximity* of nonprofits to the residents of an area can serve as a strategic advantage in terms of being able to respond in a timely and meaningful fashion to the immediate concerns of the people. Being located near markets enables nonprofits to be effective as local barometers. Their ability to accumulate knowledge and information pertaining to a local area has undoubtedly been facilitated by their physical presence in the same geographical locale as the groups they serve.

Participating in and orchestrating activities such as neighborhood canvassing drives, community meetings, and fund-raisers has given the firms significant opportunities to engage residents in informal settings. Nonprofit firms' experiences with informal community events can provide other sector participants with a reasonable comfort level as it relates to the need to effectively communicate plans to enhance local schools. Being able to collaborate with organizations that have an established rapport in an area can allay potential fear or skepticism as it relates to newcomers or outsiders who aim to change how schools operate. The *relationships and networks* that many nonprofits have formed with local citizen groups and organizations should be advantageous for collaborative partners seeking to build trust within a community. The mere presence of a trusted and tried community partner in a prospective collaborative can be a determining factor regarding whether a community's stakeholders embrace unfamiliar organizations in their school reform efforts.

This sector's ability to serve as *local implementers* of programs that are funded by federal government or nationally based private companies is a real advantage. In this role, nonprofits not only achieve greater effectiveness and efficiencies but resolve a host of logistical and operational concerns. For instance, federal agencies would no longer have to set up satellite offices or task forces to manage local programs. Similarly, a multinational company seeking to roll out products or services in a local market could utilize the expertise of a nonprofit that is firmly established in an area. The integrity, trust, and effectiveness associated with a local enterprise can basically determine the degree to which community groups accept innovative ideas about improving schools. As this sector has become increasingly knowledgeable about and experienced in local market demographics, the public and private sectors are relying more on it to execute programs on the ground; this has helped to eliminate implementation challenges that commonly plague the efforts of public and private firms.

Nationally based financial institutions sometimes work with regional banks and community development financial institutions (CDFIs) to navigate local market financial intricacies; this enables them to serve their customer bases more effectively. By partnering with local financial institutions, larger financial concerns have been able to tailor products and services in ways that make sense for distinct customer groups. Major corporations occasionally funnel their charitable contributions through these same community development financial institutions. The nonprofit community's capacity to translate large-scale projects into smaller, more manageable and localized tasks is an illustration of how it facilitates the work of the other sectors. Nonprofits' ability to customize goods and services for specific markets allows them to complement the work of other sectors in areas that may have seemed elusive in the past. This type of complementary role is a reflection of the sector's potential to lead in the development of strategies and programs that work well for all organizations involved.

EXAMPLES OF NONPROFIT PARTICIPATION IN CSC

Nonprofit institutions are crucial to the development of productive, healthy, and sustainable communities. As board members and program committees make decisions regarding the character of their portfolios, the need to address deficiencies in local schools is a growing priority. Although there may not be a critical mass of nonprofits that are engaged in tangible programs that address the transformation of elementary and secondary schools, large numbers of these entities have begun to consider what would be the most effective approaches to achieving measurable impact in education reform. For example, forming a charter school has been one course of action taken by some nonprofits as an effective response to low-performing schools. Because of the flexibility in some charter school legislation and the availability of public funding to operate charter schools, this is a viable option for many nonprofits that have limited funding available for expanding their programming into new areas, such as education. The SEED Foundation (School for Educational Evolution and Development), a national nonprofit, opened the first public boarding school in Washington, DC, and Columbia University in New York City opened a private elementary school that was originally designed to help recruit faculty with young children but ultimately was expanded to serve the youth in the surrounding community.

Whatever the path chosen, by partnering with community development corporations, churches, businesses, and governmental agencies, nonprofits can lead in the creation of practicable approaches to resolving public school dilemmas. The Public Education & Business Coalition (PEBC) in Denver, Colorado, is a nonprofit partnership comprised of educators, business leaders, and members of the local community who focus on whole-school reform. Other nonprofit collaborations include Johns Hopkins University's partnership with the City of Baltimore's school system to form the Baltimore Talent Development High School; the University of Pennsylvania's Penn Alexander School; and Stanford University's charter school, East Palo Alto High School.

Building from their competence as a type of local barometer, some nonprofits may discover that school management companies are pursuing partnerships with firms that possess knowledge of and experience with groups in local communities. In this regard, the private company may wish to take advantage of a nonprofit's expertise by hiring it as a consultant or forming a partnership with it wherein the nonprofit acts as a local area advisor. Once again, an organization's accumulated information, knowledge, and access to a community can be translated into a strategic opportunity for it to become engaged in reforming schools. There are numerous examples of how private managers of public schools have failed because they did not understand or consider the interests of the critical stakeholders in communities. A different kind of advantage for nonprofits relates to the work of social service and public-health organizations. These professionals possess skills and knowledge in domestic and social areas that have been difficult for educators to interpret and manage. By collaborating with persons who understand the impact of family and environmental issues on students' performances, partners can acquire answers to some of the more intractable dilemmas in school-age education.

A large number of nonprofit institutions should discover that they are attractive partners to institutions from other sectors because they can successfully implement local programs and services. The logistical challenges confronting a federal agency that is attempting to implement an innovative reading or math program across many states can lead the agency to the realization that it may be more productive to solicit guidance from a local entity that has some form of infrastructure already in place. By owning buildings or having access to uniquely skilled personnel, nonprofits potentially offer an easy solution to some of the more difficult challenges in school reform (i.e., securing facilities and hiring qualified personnel). Likewise, a technology firm that is seeking to donate technology services and equipment to schools throughout the country is more than likely going to solicit the input of locally established institutions in its push to elevate the technological infrastructure of school operations. CSC enables the partnering of technology firms with nonprofits at the local level as a means of providing more advanced education options for youth in varied communities.

A separate opportunity for nonprofits in CSC is their capacity to serve as a flow-through funding enterprise for federal government educational initiatives or even foundation grants that are intended to benefit youth across the country. As a local designee of a federal agency, nonprofits can be entrusted with dispensing large sums of money to persons and organizations that they deem credible and capable of providing defined services. For example, the National Science Foundation granted more than $30 million over several years to public colleges, universities, and school districts across the state of Georgia to help facilitate collaborations between schoolteachers and science and mathematics college professors. Postsecondary institutions can be instrumental in not only training and recruiting elementary and secondary instructors for schools but also initiating collaborative teaching relationships between their own faculty members and public school personnel. Nonprofits can play a meaningful role in CSC because of their strong legacy in local implementation as well as their established trust and integrity in local communities.

NONPROFIT DILEMMA: STAYING TRUE TO ITS ROOTS

One of the perennial challenges confronting nonprofit institutions is limited funding, which often translates into limited opportunities for program expansion. The desire to make a difference in neighborhoods and communities seems to always be tempered by the reality that there are never enough resources. Achieving a proper balance between addressing the most critical needs of constituents and investing funds effectively is a consistent test of institutional coherence and rationality. Another difficult task for nonprofits lies in managing the competing interests of stakeholders whose power and influence are undeniable and may reverberate throughout an organization. The influence of stakeholders can be complicated by the fact that some board members are the founders of an organization or its primary benefactors. Unlike the private sector, it has no real market accountability and therefore no need to maintain a healthy level of independence and accountability from key stakeholder groups. Moreover, there are no private market pressures, checks and balances, or incentives to ensure that a nonprofit is actually investing in the most cost-beneficial or profitable venture. If a stakeholder makes a strong enough suggestion regarding interest in a program, then the program will most likely become a funding priority. Nonprofit officers regularly incorporate varying degrees of checks and balances into their routine operations to achieve some degree of organizational integrity and credibility in the eyes of their internal and external stakeholders.

In a situation where competing stakeholders prefer different program investments, the unenviable task of the officers is to reach a workable outcome that placates the majority of stakeholders. Although the rule in most organizations is that there are always winners and losers when managing limited resources and competing interests, the hope is that over time the desires of all parties can be achieved to some degree and that the funding choices can become balanced across their varying interests. The experiences of many nonprofits reflect the need to forego individual preferences to accomplish the greater work of the organization. Where this has not been the focus, the result has been organizational fallout as extreme as the resignation of officers and as minimal as ongoing internal conflicts and power struggles. The need to remain committed to an organization's central purpose has to be balanced against impending enticements to engage in uncharted areas that may only serve to appease certain constituencies at the expense of broader, more important stakeholder concerns.

The risk of becoming so large that organizational effectiveness is lost is a very real concern for nonprofits and should serve as a constant reminder of how important it is to be keenly aware of organizational competencies in the face of new and appealing opportunities. The temptation to engage in alliances or pursue prospects to broaden an organization's portfolio can ultimately compromise the work of an enterprise if not carefully managed. Although building alliances with other firms can be a viable strategic option, engaging in partnerships that are not closely aligned with the primary activities of a nonprofit can have a diluting effect on the overall agenda. For example, where nonprofits may serve as local implementers or funding entities for larger enterprises, the expectations and parameters of the relationship can be so vague that neither party knows at what point the partnership actually ends. This can be tricky, especially when the completion stages of a venture last for several years. A multiyear relationship between firms must be managed judiciously from initiation to completion to bring proper closure to the deal. Ultimately, though, a nonprofit will want to ensure that it does not dedicate an unreasonable amount of its time and resources toward a venture that is ancillary to its mission.

The consistent theme underlying many of the imminent challenges that lie ahead for members of the nonprofit community is how to remain true to their original plans and purposes in the face of new risks and opportunities. Related to this is how to effectively maintain a healthy distinction between the nature of a nonprofit and that of a private enterprise. Although it is true that both types of firms are increasingly producing and distributing similar goods and services, the distinction remains that nonprofits do not retain profits for subsequent distribution to shareholders as dividends. The absence of stock market pressures that accompany private enterprise is a differentiating factor that allows nonprofit entities to freely offer goods and services that are most suitable to their clients. Without being concerned about whether a product or service is cost beneficial or profitable, nonprofits are often in a better position to meet the unique needs of specific market segments. Being free from capital market fluctuations and accountability does play a part in allowing these firms to stay true to their roots. Where there is responsible oversight and management by the board of directors and the executive officers, a nonprofit organization can achieve consistency in the implementation and ongoing reinterpretation of its mission in new and evolving contexts such as education reform.

7

MAXIMIZING STAKEHOLDER VALUE IN EDUCATION

THE WAVE OF PRIVATE ENTERPRISE IN PUBLIC EDUCATION

The private sector's role in our economy is largely viewed in terms of its capacity to produce, market, and distribute an array of products and services in the marketplace. The sector's accountability to the private interests of a number of stakeholder groups, such as stockholders, customers, employees, and directors, distinguishes it from other sectors, mainly because of its emphasis on retaining profits for distribution as dividends to its shareholders. Private-sector firms, to a large extent, are industrial and service companies, financial institutions, media firms, accounting and consulting firms, and a host of other small- and medium-size entities that typically earn a profit via transactions and exchanges in the marketplace. The utilization of systems and processes that lead to management and operational efficiencies establishes many distinctive competencies for private enterprises. The sector's capacity to provide goods and services that add value to practically every sphere of our lives makes it an indispensable component of the overall economy.

Its ability to respond to our private needs as consumers as well as the private interests of its stakeholders while creating financial returns reflects the essence of private enterprise. Every production, distribution, marketing, and operational decision must not only make good organizational sense but contribute to an acceptable financial result. Although the sector's capacity to produce substantial earnings and capital gains for its shareholders is viewed by some as widening the economic gap in society, the reality is that consumers cannot live without many of the goods and services being provided to them by private industry. Moreover, although we would prefer a market system that spreads the economic wealth more evenly across groups and classes, it makes more sense for us to devise solutions to this uneven wealth distribution by encouraging information and resource sharing that can move us closer to world-class public schools that almost guarantee academic success across more groups of students.

One approach is to create ways in which private industry can collaborate with the other sectors in efforts to share ideas and resources that can lead to greater equity and access for more people. Through communication and interaction, we can produce effective schools that will prepare greater numbers of young people to share in the intellectual and wealth exchange that ultimately creates value and wealth for more consumers. We cannot dismantle the private markets on the basis that a few continue to get wealthier at the expense of many. There are simply too many market efficiencies and effective systems throughout the private sector for us to ignore and not utilize in transforming school organizations and systems. For example, the unwillingness of private firms to expend resources in areas that are not compatible with their internal capacities or strategic objectives can be useful guidance for institutions considering strategic partnerships and alliances. Additionally, the private sector's ability to develop mechanisms and systems that provide timely and accurate information regarding the effectiveness of operations can provide partnerships with the tools necessary for measuring impact and determining the location of inefficiencies. Perhaps the sector's greatest asset is that it understands how to manage an enterprise and utilize internal and external resources, which is an advantage that can enhance any collaboration of organizations.

One increasing phenomenon in education reform is that many private entrepreneurs and companies are creating a range of programs, initiatives, and school prototypes that they believe address many of the critical weaknesses of elementary and secondary education. The advantage of these developments is that many nontraditional professionals and organizations are personally and professionally committed to the revamping of our schools. Through the use of knowledge and experience attained via the private production and distribution of goods and services, this sector can assist other CSC partners in developing innovative schools and programs that utilize many private-industry distinctive competencies. The sector's ultimate contribution to CSC stems from the expertise, resources, and ideas that have become staples of private-industry activities. Many of its systems, tools, and structures carry great potential for transforming public education. Those who continue to oppose any form of private-sector presence in public education are basically creating a healthy forum for examining the roles of all sectors in the transformation of our schools.

The capacity for private companies and individuals to fund new ventures in education reform is enhanced by the wealth and expertise that have been acquired via private enterprise and other related capital markets activities. Although some critics of the sector believe that greed and power dominate the mind-sets of its practitioners and entrepreneurs, most people in business are committed to donating reasonable portions of their wealth to causes that are important to them personally or professionally. Aside from the public's schizophrenia as it relates to their views about private companies, there is a whole lot of good emanating from this sector. Although many complain about the financial excesses of private companies, we must acknowledge that we are actually the ones contributing to the excess through our consumption and investment habits. Public perception regarding what drives capitalists is often distorted and unfair to a large degree. The sins of a few members are spoiling the good deeds of the majority of the other entities that make up the professions and industries. If we allow ourselves to move beyond the stereotypes and prejudgments that are shaping our opinions about private enterprise, then perhaps we can utilize the strengths of this sector and witness a metamorphosis in how we manage and operate public schools.

Corporate altruism in education enhances a company's role as a responsible community institution and allows it to contribute to the academic training of prospective workers. As companies face shrinking philanthropic budgets, there is a mandate to be more strategic in terms of how external contributions are invested. Ensuring that recipients' interests are aligned with the goals of the donor company is an increasingly prominent concern for executives. Related to this is the reality that investment in the education of future workers makes the most strategic sense when one considers how a company will sustain itself organizationally and competitively. This does not imply that companies are ceasing to contribute to social, artistic, and sports interests because donations in these areas do a lot to ensure that a company or entrepreneur maintains its stakeholder and customer relations as well as its competitive advantage. As the demographics of the marketplace continue to shift abroad, corporate executives must ensure that they employ highly trained workers whose skills are transferable across markets and cultures. Participating in the reform of public schools is one solution for ensuring that future employees are prepared to operate in a global and diverse marketplace.

Profit maximization is clearly a dichotomy for private-sector participants because it is both a necessary barometer for organizational decision making and a hindrance when engaging in nontraditional ventures such as CSC, where profit maximization may not be a priority at all. In making the appropriate determinations about market opportunities, executives must adhere to financial and managerial goals and targets that dictate the terms by which new ventures are to be measured. This type of financial discipline ensures that coherence and consistency are maintained throughout an organization. Without clearly defined parameters, many private companies could find themselves not well positioned in the eyes of consumers and the financial markets and thus not perceived as being competitive in the marketplace. The establishment of company-wide strategic, production, marketing, and financial plans provides benchmarks for all ancillary decision making that takes place at all managerial levels. This effectively creates synergies across the divisions of a company as well as throughout the product and service portfolios being offered to consumers.

With respect to private-sector participation in CSC, the parameters traditionally employed when making determinations about investments and new products will not always apply, because of the unique characteristics surrounding the delivery of public education. There will undoubtedly be instances whereby the systems or services required to adequately address the learning needs of some students will warrant expending dollars in areas where one may not be able to quantify the benefits. Many learning tools and mechanisms may not lend themselves to being measurable or quantifiable in ways that private companies are accustomed. In this regard, partners will have to trust that the application of these tools and systems will produce the desirable outcomes. For example, maintaining a specified teacher–pupil ratio requires the hiring of additional faculty whose salaries may not appear to be cost effective from the perspective of a private-industry professional. Although the benefits of added faculty may not be readily quantifiable, the long-run effects of this type of teaching approach are expected to enhance student academic performance, thereby yielding higher standardized-test scores.

The differentiating characteristics of public education explain why it will be important to temper the focus on maximizing profits when examining CSC options for school reform. By ignoring what is unique about school operations and administration, partners can jeopardize the vision and outcomes of a partnership. By gathering critical masses of data and information, CSC partners can accommodate the need to produce measurable results under different circumstances. The ways of doing business in private industry can seem crass and illegitimate when one is not familiar with or accustomed to preestablished financial and strategic goals and targets. Cost-cutting recommendations in areas of public education may cause great alarm for those who may not completely understand how to operate a school efficiently. The information sharing and learning that can occur via CSC is intended to illustrate for traditional educators how to incorporate nontraditional processes (e.g., management tools and systems) into the infrastructure of a school. There is unlimited potential for how we can import the best of the sector's strategies, structures, and systems to enhance the overall delivery of public education.

PRIVATE-SECTOR ROLES IN CSC

Senior executives in private industry rely on *strategic planning* to establish a concrete road map for fulfilling the missions of their organizations.

Pursuant to this planning process, officers of a company delineate financial goals, target markets, short- and long-term objectives, market opportunities, distribution channels, and various other aspects of the company's planned operations and business activities. As mentioned previously, strategic planning exercises instill a degree of corporate discipline into the management of private entities. They are a means for setting parameters and goals by which individual managers are evaluated and held accountable by their superiors. As a partner in CSC, private-sector companies and professionals can lead the others in developing appropriate road maps for a school prototype or for overhauling the systems and structures of an existing school. As a type of *strategic barometer*, private companies and entrepreneurs can lead in the formulation of plans that make sense in the context of a community's needs. By accounting for the local knowledge, influence, and experiences of its religious and nonprofit cohorts, private-sector participants can facilitate the creation of relevant strategic and organizational plans. The actual collaboration of the individuals and institutions from the different sectors should result in plans and programs that incorporate the strengths and distinctive competencies of the respective sectors. Realistically, the role of private-sector practitioners can be to serve as a strategic guide for integrating the various ideas and recommendations of each entity. This can help a venture adhere to a degree of coherence and consistency between what a community's interests are regarding local schools and the eventual strategies for addressing the community's school concerns.

The *management proficiency* that often characterizes this sector is an advantage to be reckoned with in CSC. Many of our schools remain ineffective simply because administrators do not understand how to effectively manage an entity and all of its components. The majority of educational administrators are trained as educators and not as organizational managers, although many schools of education have incorporated managerial-type courses into their curricula as a means of preparing future teachers in these areas. For many teaching professionals and educational administrators, there exists an operational vacuum as they grapple with how to effectively integrate and navigate across the teaching, learning, and operational spheres of a school while attempting to create synergies along the way. Private companies have proven to be adept at producing synergies across diverse systems and units that compose an organization. In fact, they are good at managing human and capital resources, without regard to whether the decisions are popular. The private-enterprise emphasis on achieving objectives such as efficient resource utilization and cost-effectiveness will undoubtedly benefit a collaborative effort. This type of management experience and proficiency should indeed assist traditional educators in shifting their focus beyond one dimension of the education process and toward the multiple components of an entire school operation.

This sector's ability to develop and implement *management systems* that facilitate timely and accurate decision making should prove to be extremely useful for a CSC experiment. Implementing different forms of administrative and operational systems into the infrastructure of a local school can transform how schools operate and educate young people. Understanding the key components of local school operations and the academic goals thereof is a key determinant for how management systems can be incorporated into the overall structure. For example, the implementation of meaningful systems for training teachers and evaluating their performance can assist school administrators in their planning for an upcoming school year. Separately, engaging in proper resource planning by aligning schoolwide expectations with the resources and systems accessible by teaching professionals can produce considerable results when evaluating the academic performance of students and whole schools. Private firms can instruct a collaboration as they seek ways of interpreting data that are gathered via management systems that are focused on areas such as administration, operations, and marketing.

Developing an appreciation for how data accumulation and reporting can enhance the effectiveness and efficiency of an organization can revolutionize how local schools are managed and operated. Private-sector emphasis on utilizing appropriate *evaluation and reporting tools* can be beneficial as CSC partners examine how to produce quantifiable results from school processes. To adequately measure the performance of a school and the academic achievement of its students, partners need to develop evaluation and reporting mechanisms that produce relevant, measurable, and monitorable data for analysis. One of the primary goals in the transformation of local schools is the creation of formats that provide key stakeholders with meaningful performance measurements. Utilizing evaluative tools that are consistent with the overall academic objectives of schools can produce the types of performance indicators needed for stakeholders to properly assess a school's performance. When financial institutions produce customer bank and credit card statements from their large and integrated databases, they essentially manipulate the data in ways that convey specific kinds of internal and external information. Finance companies can share this kind of expertise with school administrators and teach them how to produce relevant reports from databases of student information. Private-sector familiarity and experience with implementing systems that are properly aligned with specified goals and objectives can be useful as collaborators seek to establish ways of measuring and monitoring the progress of their school initiatives.

The *results orientation* of private companies can be important, especially in light of the prevailing trend toward accountability and standards in the education industry. The existing momentum for students to meet standardized-testing benchmarks is one reason why a great deal of emphasis should be placed on accumulating measurable and monitorable results. In the larger public arena, there is an intense desire to see meaningful performance measurements that indicate to the public that local schools are working once again. Because so many private companies are held accountable to the interests of varied stakeholder groups, they are in a unique position to inform their cocollaborators about the types of reporting that can produce the kinds of data, information, and reports that the public is calling for. By collaborating with educators and others, private-sector professionals can lead in the establishment and maintenance of a focus on concrete performance indicators that effectively communicate to the public how well or not local school ventures are performing.

The *integration of technology* into aspects of teaching and learning can elevate the entire education process. Similar to private companies, schools must continue to acknowledge the integral role that information and technology play as we progress through this century. As a CSC partner, private firms can continue to demonstrate the technological benefits that are available to local schools, by performing online or customized demonstrations for administrators and classroom instructors. CSC partners should invite local technology firms to join the partnership to gain the advantages from this type of expertise and knowledge.

There are innumerable technology companies that would be willing and excited about consulting with schools on a pro bono basis regarding the integration of software and hardware applications into the education of school-age children. The importance of technology in education must be emphasized in any CSC initiative that is being designed to transform the overall educational experiences of young people. Private-sector entities are in the best position to offer insight into the most effective ways to utilize technology in educational management and operations.

EXAMPLES OF PRIVATE-SECTOR PARTICIPATION IN CSC

Private-sector involvement in the reform of local schools is taking a variety of forms. What is interesting about this multiplicity is that companies and professionals are engaging themselves in varying degrees and seemingly in accordance with the unique needs of their local communities. An encouraging observation related to corporate involvement is that the companies recognize that there are tremendous opportunities to become involved in the academic training of their future employees and managers. Consistent with their goals of maintaining strategic consistency, many firms target school programs within their service areas or initiate programs that build from the skills and interests of their existing personnel. The strategic options for entrepreneurs and companies are vast and allow for company-specific interpretation regarding how to effectively respond to the local dilemmas in school-age education. Because the problems are difficult to pinpoint, the market is wide open for private entities and individuals to enter the education industry and provide much-needed leadership and instruction in key areas of educational management and operations. An example is Victory Schools, a private education management and consulting company that manages public schools and school districts in New York and Philadelphia.

By adopting a local school, many companies are able to develop an ongoing relationship with a school and participate in the revamping of school processes that may not be functioning well. This approach allows companies and their professionals to provide long-term consistent expertise that is intended to enhance targeted areas such as assessment and administration. By adopting a school for a period of time, companies are able to determine whether the academic performance of the students and the school is actually improving as a result of their intervention. This strategy carries an ancillary benefit because it can enhance a company's profile in the community as a good, responsible corporate citizen. The opportunities for maintaining and expanding the customer base are not lost either, because consumers are always more inclined to patronize companies that share their values and concerns. To advance their social profiles even further, private entities should consider collaborating with local institutions from the other sectors.

Building a school from the ground up has been an opportunity for a company to customize a school in its own image. Based on individual company views and observations about what school-age education should entail, school prototypes are being developed to reflect sketchy and comprehensive approaches to education. Although some of these on-site customized schools have been established so that employees' children may attend schools near their parents' workplaces, others serve students in surrounding communities. Honeywell, Inc., partnered with the city of Niagara Falls, New York, to build the new Niagara Falls High School. The corporation raised more than $80 million on Wall Street to build the school and leased it back to the school district. Separately, an example of a workplace charter school is the Renaissance Elementary Charter School in Miami, which was originally created for the children of Ryder System, Inc., employees, but has since expanded its reach to include children whose parents work for other companies. As corporate philanthropists are confronted with the mandate to develop plans that accommodate several corporate objectives simultaneously, school customizing can be a way to enhance the lives of community constituents, as well as prospective workers.

A different version of the customized school is the decision by a group of firms to engage in a cooperative school effort. A joint initiative among private entities can be extended to include firms and persons representing the nonprofit, religious, and public sectors as well. In my view, the broader the cooperative, the greater the likelihood of incorporating the views and recommendations of a broader section of a community. Likewise, greater participation would mitigate the possibility of overloading a few firms with a large amount of responsibility. A school cooperative is actually a precursor to CSC as it can originate from the idea that partnerships can be effective means of participating in external projects that may not be central to the operations of an organization. This type of venture can also communicate to local citizens that there is a critical mass of interest in making educational opportunities better for the youth of a community.

Mentoring programs continue to garner widespread interest and participation among professionals across many industries. Accounting, financial, legal, professional sports, consulting, and technology industries are a few whose workers consistently participate in company-sponsored programs designed to lead and assist school-age children as they move through grade school. One opportunity in CSC is to develop a type of mentoring clearinghouse or headquarters that assigns personnel from all sectors to schools throughout a region. This vehicle would enable large numbers of professionals to work directly with youth while sharing their knowledge and experiences. Mentoring relationships can be effective because they accommodate young people's needs to learn from persons who are working in an industry that may be a career interest. The impact on a young mind of being able to observe a mentor's daily routine and receive firsthand guidance cannot be underestimated.

Some wealthy entrepreneurs have chosen to underwrite scholarship programs for targeted groups of youngsters in a single market or in multiple regions across the country. These programs are often accomplished through a voucher arrangement that allows students to transfer from poorly performing public schools to private, parochial, or independent schools. Within the framework of CSC, individuals and organizations that are funding educational costs can partner with institutions from the other sectors as a means of tapping into their local knowledge about specific groups of students in communities. Community organizations and leaders can offer invaluable insight, especially as it relates to communicating the availability of scholarships and the selection of scholarship recipients. Funding scholarships is significant, especially in situations where parents cannot afford to pay for private school tuition and other related costs. Although the programs typically benefit only a fraction of a student population, it is important to acknowledge that the funding entrepreneur or organization is making a substantial contribution to improving educational opportunities for young people.

As a way of responding to the lifestyle needs of employees, private firms are offering comprehensive child-care services before and after school hours as well as during school breaks and school closings. The work schedules of many professionals are so diverse and unpredictable that numerous employers have determined that an investment in on-site child-care services can directly affect the productivity of their employees. Company-owned child-care facilities are basically an extension of efforts to address some of the personal and family needs of workers whose professional requirements are expanding beyond an eight-hour day. Providing quality services that consist of activities such as tutoring, recreational programs, nutritious meals, academic coaching, and homework assistance creates an atmosphere that complements the in-school routine of students. This approach is a necessary service for working parents who want to ensure that their children have access to meaningful care outside of regular school hours. A CSC alliance can accommodate a private company's interest in providing this range of child-care services because the company would need to partner with a number of outside firms to acquire services such as transportation, tutoring, food, and volunteers.

Another area of opportunity for the private sector is to offer consulting services for school management, operations, and administration or to simply be an avenue for the outsourcing of these functions. As has been illustrated, there is enormous potential for consultants to collaborate with others regarding the improvement of school processes. Technology and operations consultants would be invaluable additions to a CSC partnership whose mission is to improve the internal processes of an existing school. Industrial engineers and workspace design consultants can transform the teaching and learning spaces within schools. The provision of pro bono consulting work continues to be an attractive means for consulting firms to perform charitable work and contribute in an area that makes good strategic sense for the firm. CSC partners should take advantage of the vast array of skills and expertise of those who work as uniquely defined consultants in their respective industries.

Persons and organizations across this sector are opening their own schools, creating uniquely designed support programs, floating bonds to raise dollars for school renovations, and building schools in exchange for commercially appealing land. David Robinson, a former professional basketball player founded, along with his wife, the Carver Academy, a K–6 school in San Antonio, Texas. The school reflects the virtues and ideals of its namesake, George Washington Carver: leadership, discipline, initiative, and integrity. Microsoft Corporation has introduced the Partners in Learning initiative, which is designed to empower teachers and students by providing access to the newest generation of computer technologies and training. The initiative consists of software investment and over $250 million in cash grants worldwide for technology skills training, curriculum development, technical support, research funding, and teacher and student resources.

PRIVATE-SECTOR MOTIVATIONS IN EDUCATION: FACT OR FICTION

An ongoing challenge confronting private-sector firms and persons who are interested in transforming schools is whether their intentions are rooted in a profit motivation or a sense of commitment to improving the educational opportunities for school-age children. Although no one has the right to judge or prejudge another's motivations, the reality is that a large percentage of the public audience believes that earning profits is what attracts most private entities to the management of public schools. As stated before, a profit motive in and of itself is not at all a bad thing; however, within the framework of school-age education, the motive may have to be tempered or put aside in favor of more noble goals such as achieving educational equity across demographic groups. To the extent that private firms and entrepreneurs are willing to accept and understand that many facets of school-age education may not fall within preestablished financial parameters, the potential for achieving greater public acceptance and consensus is enhanced. By communicating to a community that the ultimate goal is to improve schools for the youth, private entities can effectively dispel and mute the skepticism and mistrust that so many harbor toward the sector as a whole.

Many of the private companies that are currently engaged in managing public schools across the country are falling short, in my view, primarily because of their need to earn profits. Further, it may be virtually impossible for a publicly traded company to simultaneously accommodate the financial interests of Wall Street analysts and the educational needs of school-age children. There are simply too many components of education that require monetary investments that will not fit within the financial model of a publicly traded company. This is not to say that the interests of both sides cannot be coincidentally met through careful planning and implementation. However, the important point is that partners in education cannot be driven primarily by a need to meet the expectations of the financial markets. Instead, the emphasis has to be placed consistently on responding to the distinguishable needs of school children in a community as defined by collaborators. If individuals and companies allow the educational priorities of children to drive an initiative, then perhaps we might witness situations that do in fact result in achieving greater efficiencies and earning profits.

Overcoming the characterizations of ethical lapses and compromises by private-sector leaders can prove to be quite a daunting task because so many observers simply do not believe that private firms can divorce themselves from the temptations of greed and unethical behavior. Because there are innumerable advantages to be gained from private-sector participation in education reform, the focus has to be shifted away from the naysayers and toward producing results that will eventually convert doubters to become supporters of education privatization in varying degrees. School privatization should not imply that the essence of public education changes; rather, it should reflect the potential of private-sector structures and systems to enhance how we deliver education to our young people. To date, the public dialogue surrounding education privatization is focused on the system of privatization, but it does not emphasize the true potential that accompanies this type of systematic change in elementary and secondary education.

Merging mores and tendencies across sectors will not be a foregone conclusion, because the respective organizations do make their choices and decisions differently. Although it is apparent to the casual observer that private-sector personnel are predisposed to a more structured and disciplined approach to decision making, it is equally evident that many of our colleagues in the nonprofit, religious, and public sectors do not at times display a propensity toward structure and timeliness in their decision making. In fact, although the private sector is often characterized as being innovative and risk prone, those operating outside of private industry are inclined to display more moderate and traditional tendencies, which are viewed as being slow and lacking in innovation. Partners from the different sectors will be charged with reconciling these disparate tendencies to develop plans and programs that improve the academic performance of students.

Ultimately, private companies and entrepreneurs will be able to silence their critics by implementing strategies, systems, and structures that will lead to positive academic results from students and schools. Posturing about the advantages of private enterprise will not suffice, especially in light of the prevailing public mistrust and skepticism about private participation in school reform. Some private managers of public schools have taken an elitist approach to school reform by displaying the attitude that they have all of the answers; as a result, many have failed miserably along the way. Many of these companies have left the education industry altogether, merged with other firms, scaled back their original plans, or shifted their focus entirely. These outcomes indicate that community stakeholders are not at all interested in companies' own high estimations of what they believe they can do in education. These stakeholder groups expect to participate fully in every aspect of planning and implementation, not to sit back and allow private companies to dictate their ideas for school change to them. Healthy levels of humility and openness will serve many of our private-sector colleagues well as they seek to engage their nonprofit-, public-, and religious-sector counterparts in CSC ventures.

8

THE QUANDARY OF THE PUBLIC SECTOR

A REBIRTH IN THE PUBLIC SECTOR

The public sector is distinguished by its role in providing public goods and services such as schools, hospitals, law enforcement, transportation, parks, and libraries. Institutions composing this sector include not only the federal, state, and local levels of government but also their affiliate agencies and departments, as well as quasi-governmental entities such as Fannie Mae and the U.S. Postal Service. Not only have many of the goods and services being provided through public enterprise become more costly, but the task of devising effective and efficient means of delivering these goods seems to be elusive for policymakers and leaders. The high levels of bureaucracy that normally characterize governmental entities are viewed primarily as hindrances to productivity and innovation. The size of federal programs is so vast that it is almost impossible to tailor them to the needs of local communities. A separate reality is that the sector's use of obsolete systems and practices in certain areas leads many observers to view it as being out of sync with the pulse of 21st-century innovation and creativity. Nevertheless, we have witnessed in recent years a sector that is attempting to reinvent and reengineer itself by incorporating systems and processes that have been employed successfully in private industry.

The sector's capacity to fill voids that remain after the nonprofit, private, and religious sectors have responded to social and economic needs of communities represents a real and tangible advantage. Because there are many private market imperfections and externalities, the hope continues to be that public-sector interventions will fill in gaps and insufficiencies. One goal of CSC is for firms and professionals to create solutions that will mitigate gaps in the distribution of and access to educational resources at the elementary and secondary levels. In its role as a type of overseer of public goods and services, our government (i.e., the public sector) attempts to implement policies that affect a broader range of groups and develop programs that are more complete than might be the case in the private markets. To achieve equity and fairness for citizens, governmental entities, in theory, are expected to serve as a type of equity barometer. Whether accomplished through direct intervention (e.g., provision of funds) or indirect measures (e.g., tax credits), the public sector has an integral role to play in devising solutions that are applicable across the entire spectrum of society.

The outrage over the deplorable state of public schools can be heard virtually from every corner of society. Although the targets of the fury are not always apparent, the consensus is that those who have been charged with delivering public education have done a poor and ineffective job for years. Without pointing fingers or even taking responsibility, public-sector leaders are attempting to be proactive by developing new guidelines and mandates that are intended to address some of the weaknesses and inadequacies in school-age education. As policymakers continue to establish new programs for ensuring that all children have equal access to a high-quality education, the overwhelming challenges continue to be how to transport these initiatives to the local levels and how to ensure that local officials receive adequate funding to implement them. Reconciling statewide implementation with federal mandates has always eluded the casual observer because what one sees put in place locally does not often line up with the lofty promises made at the federal level. Indeed, the disparities are often the result of insufficient funding at the state and local levels, as is justifiably argued by many administrators and teachers.

The implementation gaps between federal and state governments reflect one of the more glaring weaknesses in school-age education.

Prospective CSC organizations and professionals will find significant opportunities to develop prototypes that can address the range of disconnects that exist between state school allocations and federal government guidelines with respect to funding and implementation in local schools. Although it is true that many states simply do not have enough funding in their annual budgets to fully implement federally sponsored initiatives, it is equally true that some states do not go far enough in their efforts to address preestablished goals and targets. The lack of effort and creativity by some state educators has essentially robbed thousands of young people of a chance for meaningful educational experiences. CSC is a viable alternative for state and local educators who may not possess the will or proficiency to implement federal initiatives. By collaborating with professionals and organizations outside of the traditional public sector, educators may discover the personnel needed to fulfill certain instructional gaps or even locate the financial resources needed to implement a particular reading program. If given a chance, CSC can replace the status quo and complacency with innovation and creativity in many aspects of public education.

Many have challenged the will and commitment of public educators from all angles and have essentially concluded that education professionals lack the capacity to serve young people adequately. Indeed, taxpayers have the right as well as the responsibility to hold public school administrators and teaching professionals accountable to the mandates that are being funded with tax dollars. However, now that we have witnessed an almost complete debacle in the academic performance of our public schools and, therefore, the students, our task is to engage ourselves about the strategies and solutions for emerging from the shambles with a fresh outlook and road map for educating our youth to lead us into the future. Even if we believe that the educational elites lack the proclivity or expertise to set our schools on the right track, our task remains that of rallying behind the education industry to assist them in changing the course that our schools have been on for too many years. Many professionals throughout the education industry have displayed a renewed willingness to engage new ideas and concepts that will help them shift gears. Those outside of the industry should view such renewed focus as an indication that educators do in fact possess enough zeal and commitment to improve schools and are also prepared to listen to the ideas and views of external stakeholders of education.

There is a tacit admission by educators that help is needed if school-age education is going to be revived. Although school administrators have not always exhibited an inclination to embrace nontraditional approaches to public school delivery, we have witnessed a gradual shift in the degree of acceptance of innovative approaches over the past decade. By allowing the implementation of varying forms of charter schools and voucher initiatives, legislators have created a platform from which CSC can build. Because some of the early results from charter and voucher experiments have shown some gains in student achievement, education decision makers are showing greater interest in the models being proposed by those outside of the industry. Albeit with extreme caution, policymakers and public school administrators have approved different types of partnerships between school districts and various organizations and professionals, with the goal being to integrate identifiable strengths and resources of businesses, foundations, and so forth, that may prove to be integral to transforming schools. By building alliances with companies and other individuals throughout local communities to provide goods and services that cannot be purchased within an operating budget, school leaders should begin to see how options such as CSC can fill some of the implementation and funding gaps between federal mandates and local funding capabilities.

The public sentiment toward innovation in how we educate our youth is consistent with that of school leaders and policymakers. Even though most people know that significant change is warranted, there is not a huge rush to completely turn over the reins of public school administration to private companies or any other organization that does not have experience in educating young people or has not proven that it can produce better academic results. The piecemeal approach seems to be the preferred mode, which has meant rolling out a new program in a limited number of grades or schools at a time or creating a manageable number of school prototypes in the short term. Proceeding with caution does seem to allow reform experimentation on a trial basis, thus avoiding risks associated with large-scale rollouts. The distinguishable features of each school environment underscore the need for community stakeholders to examine closely the unique learning needs of students in their respective areas. CSC can be a solution for communities as they attempt to identify which elements within local schools warrant improvement or, perhaps, complete overhaul.

Although it has taken a strong push from those outside of the education arena, the public sector is on a course that will lead to a major reengineering of how public education is delivered at the elementary and secondary levels. The astronomical amounts of money that we have expended toward public schools over the past decades indicate to us that the areas requiring a revamping may not necessarily be more costly but merely require completely different systems or methodologies of teaching and learning. Although some aspects will surely cost substantial money (e.g., facilities renovation, technology integration, and tailored learning programs), we will undoubtedly witness cost efficiencies in some facets of school-age education before it is all said and done. Recognition by educators that we can no longer rely on ineffective and outdated teaching and learning approaches is allowing us to integrate fresh concepts and models that should be able to produce significant improvements in the academic performance of our youth. By collaborating with persons and institutions from other industries and professions, public-sector leaders will discover that there are enormous amounts of untapped resources and expertise that can be useful for improving our local schools.

PUBLIC-SECTOR ROLES IN CSC

The primary role of public enterprise is to guarantee that all children have equal access to a high-quality education. The citizenry expects this sector to serve as a type of *equity barometer* to ensure that governmental spending adequately accounts for the educational needs of young people everywhere. Although federal government mandates do not always appear to be equitable and fair in practice, the goal is always to establish the most complete directives for state and local officials to follow. As in many instances of federal government policymaking, the challenge continues to revolve around implementation and monitoring at the state and local levels. Although our legislators seek to enact fairly reasonable targets and timetables that promise the best for every child, the proper controls and monitoring tools are often not applied to ensure that these expectations become realities in local communities. Within CSC, there is the potential to partner with state and local education organizations and professionals who possess local knowledge and experience and who can assist in the monitoring and delivery of federal government directives. Public-sector experiences and insight regarding the learning needs of groups of students will be invaluable as CSC partners design, implement, and monitor new models that respond to learning challenges facing students across the country. The combination of educators' knowledge and access at the federal and local levels can close some of the gaps that are hindering their capacity to implement new programs and gauge their progress.

As the *ultimate overseer and provider of public education*, public enterprise has the responsibility to examine the range of innovative proposals for school reform and to select and implement those that offer the best opportunities to enhance academic achievement. Educators have perhaps an unintended mandate from taxpayers to explore the entire range of system- and market-based reform options in the marketplace without regard to the types of organizations leading the reform efforts. Because so many schools are suffering, the public is demanding and anticipating major changes in many places, which include the adoption of nontraditional approaches to school reform. This means that many traditionalists and educational elites will be challenged with respect to their roles and perspectives about how public education should be delivered. As overseer, this sector must simultaneously protect what is unique about schools and ensure that school administration is not turned upside down or inside out solely for the sake of reform. Careful planning in collaboration with institutional and individual partners from other sectors can achieve the best solutions for individual communities while preserving the uniqueness of public schools and adopting innovative approaches that can propel school-age education to new heights.

The *substantial underwriting potential* of this sector can basically determine the degree to which any meaningful reform occurs. Because development and implementation costs are usually in the millions (if not billions) of dollars, new education initiatives are most often funded by our government, which has the capacity to appropriate large amounts from the federal budget. Federally sponsored academic programs that are accompanied by adequate financial resources are more likely to achieve the desired outcomes upon implementation at the state and local levels. For example, to achieve targeted standardized-test scores, states and school districts must receive the funding and support necessary to administer programs needed for preparing the students. Legislative vehicles such as loans, grants, tax incentives, and tax credits represent important financing opportunities that can be awarded by the public sector to firms and individuals who are interested in school improvements. These kinds of funding alternatives can close budget gaps for schools and make underfunded initiatives affordable and feasible. Despite the deep pockets of our government, a consistent challenge is reconciling the application of millions of dollars with the need to observe quantifiable change in academic performance.

Coupled with the capacity to provide different funding and financing options, this sector's accumulated experiences in education are indispensable. The *public school knowledge and expertise* of professionals and organizations in education are a distinct advantage for public enterprises. Within CSC, nonprofit-, private-, and religious-sector participants should discover how critical it will be to have seasoned educators on their team, primarily because they usually possess knowledge and insight regarding public school teaching, learning, operations, and administration. Although traditional educators may not offer innovative solutions to many of the operational, administrative, and logistical challenges in school-age education, their expertise in other areas is matchless. Components such as curriculum development and special-needs learning require the perspectives and inputs of professionals who have been trained to work in these areas. Additionally, pedagogical and child development concerns appear to be well beyond the professional domain of those who have not been properly trained to interpret the intricacies surrounding these aspects of education.

EXAMPLES OF PUBLIC-SECTOR PARTICIPATION IN CSC

As public-sector professionals and organizations engage their counterparts from the nonprofit, private, and religious communities, one of their primary responsibilities should be to preserve the character and integrity of elementary and secondary education. In so doing, educators must ensure that others comprehend and carefully consider elements in education that may not appear to be cost beneficial but are nonetheless critical for meeting the larger goals of teaching and learning. For example, costly educational features such as special-needs instruction, smaller classroom sizes, and comprehensive curricula have been deemed integral to the overall education of young people and therefore cannot be sacrificed or eliminated because they do not fit within a certain financial model. Another key feature in education that must be examined carefully in CSC is achieving the proper mix between well-trained teaching professionals and paraprofessionals. Collaborators must avoid the temptation to employ paraprofessionals solely because they are cheaper to hire. Educators must not compromise the academic training of our youth by allowing themselves or their collaborators to become fixated on financial models and predetermined targets. The integrity of public education demands that we expend the necessary resources to ensure that we offer our young people the best opportunities to succeed in school. Educators must lead their CSC partners in devising plans that will incorporate the unique fundamentals of public schools and advance some of the inventive ideas about transforming schools, sometimes without regard to cost.

Administrators and teaching professionals know best how to run schools and teach students. Just as private companies and entrepreneurs have discovered, participants in school reform must recognize the importance of working with experienced educators to develop prototypes and other learning enhancements. Companies that are contracting to run schools regularly invite former or current school superintendents to join them in senior administrative or executive roles. There are also numerous examples of charter schools being formed by experienced administrators or teachers who choose to take their years of knowledge and expertise and convert them into their own vision for school reform. Despite the unique contributions of professionals from outside of the education industry, educators are especially qualified and trained to inform everyone else about school-age education. For example, they understand age and grade differences and how to design instructional activities to meet learning objectives. In CSC, educators' expertise in all areas pertaining to classroom instruction and pedagogy can provide a strong foundation from which to build school improvement models. Their training and firsthand experiences with teaching children can help to maintain what is special about classroom experiences and local school operations.

Administrators' familiarity with the operational and logistical activities of local school settings can provide direction for others who are attempting to develop prototypes or systemic enhancements. As firms and individuals who are new to education make decisions about school security, food service, or transportation, they should draw on the perspectives and experiences of school administrators. For example, companies that may be proposing to extend school days may want to consult with those who can provide insight into how such a proposal might be logistically accomplished. Separately, decisions to outsource food services or student transportation should probably be made after working through how these changes might affect routine school operations and activities. CSC should expose a range of options for collaborators to incorporate the skills and expertise of those who have been trained to teach students and manage schools. The roles for teaching professionals and school administrators are critical to the success of any venture that will be formed to enhance student learning.

Within the CSC framework, there are a variety of ways in which the federal government can continue to partner with its state- and local-level counterparts in the rollout of education programs. Federal guidelines in reading and math can be transported to individual states and across school districts by working with state education departments to successfully implement and monitor the programs. Legislative appropriations for facilities acquisitions or renovations can be allocated across states with the assistance of state and local enterprises. CSC will provide additional advantages as public entities discover the range of skills and resources held by persons and organizations representing the nonprofit, private, and religious communities. Collaboration across sectors, with the intent to improve local schools, bears unlimited potential for exposing creative and innovative solutions to many school dilemmas that have seemed to be virtually intractable.

FROM RESISTANCE TO ACKNOWLEDGMENT: A WILLINGNESS TO CHANGE

As public-sector professionals and organizations continue to grapple with and sometimes resist the change that is imminent in school-age education, they must confront a range of fears and obstacles that have plagued the industry for decades. The unprecedented interest in local school reform by firms and individuals representing virtually every sector, profession, and industry of society will either include the public sector in the groundswell or overtake it. Major changes in elementary and secondary education are on the horizon, and the public sector must determine that it will embrace the changes or be left wanting in the end. The interests of nonprofit, private, and religious entities in education should not be viewed as anathema but must be seen as opportunities for enhancing the quality of education for all youth. Although we are witnessing signs that educators are willing and committed to change, there are equally signs of resistance and complacency that can threaten the chances for improvement in some communities that desperately need it.

Although many in this sector may harbor a justifiable sense of territorialism about their local schools, we must create effective means of communicating and engaging one another to enable a greater sense of trust, sharing, and exchange. Implicit in this goal is the need to avoid finger-pointing, to establish and maintain a focus on improving schools and the academic achievement of young people. Collaboration in education is an opportunity to move beyond the boundaries that have separated sectors, industries, and professions and to focus on how all entities can contribute to the development of effective schools in communities across the nation. Perhaps, one of the greatest threats to the effectiveness of CSC is the unwillingness of some to embrace significant change. Although we have placed administrators and teaching professionals as stewards over the education of young people, we are ultimately all shareholders of public education. The fiduciary responsibility of public school stewards and taxpayers is to openly embrace what each has to offer as we move closer to reinventing schools for all children.

The impact of politics, bureaucracy, and nepotism in this sector has been strong and almost impenetrable in some communities. Although one cannot expect to completely eliminate these types of interests and influences, their impact on decision making in education must be tempered and managed in ways that contribute to the overall enhancement of public schools. The roles of politicians, teachers unions, and many other special interest groups are crucial in setting education policy; however, they cannot be allowed to dictate decision making at the expense of what is optimal for educating our youth at the highest levels. Implicit in CSC is the potential to dilute the influence of a few stalwarts by the participation of persons and organizations from other sectors; this will likely bring new and inventive ideas to the table that may challenge pet programs or recycled plans that have not produced positive academic outcomes for years.

Indeed, it is no secret that the largest portion of every education dollar is being spent on administrative costs as opposed to classroom activities. There has to be a major realignment of expenditures to begin the process of school transformation. For example, this will require making tough decisions to eliminate administrative positions that do not have an identifiable impact on academic goals. The performance of educators must be reconciled with their compensation, to elicit the most bang for a buck. Further, steps must be taken to rid school systems of those who lack a reasonable level of commitment to the ideals and goals of high-quality education. As we continue to elevate the teaching profession in terms of compensation and training requirements, we must apply greater scrutiny and engage in careful evaluation of those whom we select as stewards over our children's education. A greater balance between pay and responsibility has to be achieved to create a meaningful platform for evaluation and performance at the school, teacher, and student levels.

Because of its capacity to respond to policy shortcomings at the state and local levels and to strategic imperfections and inefficiencies in other sectors, the public sector has an indispensable role to play in the reinvention of schools. Where cities and states may lack a road map for guiding their schools to academic productivity, education leaders at the federal level possess the capacity to establish the necessary standards and performance guidelines. This type of intergovernmental collaboration is an essential foundation for what CSC can offer decision makers as they strive to transform local schools. This sector's strengths and assets, combined with the wide-ranging resources and expertise of the nonprofit, private, and religious sectors, can lead to the transformation of schools that is desperately needed in so many communities across the nation. By collaborating with professionals and organizations of other sectors about improving the performance of students and schools, public-sector entities should begin to witness positive academic results and a concurrent dismantling of the complacency and status quo mentality that often characterize the sector.

9

CONCLUDING THOUGHTS

The range of school reform options being presented to families and communities poses new and challenging queries whose resolutions will undoubtedly lead to innovative and nontraditional choices. Although the preeminent concerns continue to be excellence in academic performance, educational equity, and freedom of choice, a number of trends and dichotomies have emerged that are causing families, educators, and other concerned citizens to adjust the lenses through which they view their education priorities. Specifically, a critical examination of whether desegregation presupposes school equity has to be made to address civil rights mandates and intentions in the context of achieving equity and excellence across the school spectrum. Likewise, each family and community will have to resolve on several levels whether a market approach or systemic approach to school reform is a viable solution for them. The perennial public-versus-private-school question remains, albeit with a twist, relating to school vouchers. The complexity surrounding these themes and the innovativeness of the reform models being proposed underscore the importance of clearly understanding and articulating our education priorities and expectations as individual communities and the nation as a whole.

No longer is the dilemma merely a choice between public and private school. The decisions are becoming more complex as families must consider the curricular versus extracurricular components of education, as well as the macro- versus microdimensions. As such, parents will be seeking a measure of confidence that their school of choice not only prepares their children intellectually and academically but also exposes and trains them in areas that integrate the increased information and technical demands of an interdisciplinary world. The collaboration of entities from the nonprofit, private, public, and religious sectors is a timely response to these types of parental concerns. The combination of ideas, resources, and expertise of persons and organizations from varied sectors can lead to teaching and learning methodologies that reflect the increased knowledge and skill requirements of our changed world. By creating forums for collaboration across sectors whose purposes are to enhance teaching and learning experiences, the intellectual, academic, technical, and artistic interests of young people can be fulfilled.

Whether the new players in the education marketplace add value to the education processes depends on the assessments of parents, communities, and any other stakeholder that chooses to participate in a collaborative local effort. Achieving the proper balance between the students' needs and what a prototype can offer is crucial as the collaborators evaluate the potential of a prospective proposal. For those parents and educators who are concerned about diversity, equity across schools, and standards and accountability, the collaboration process may seem uncommonly intricate and cumbersome. Although CSC is potentially the best solution for transforming schools in particular communities, managing and integrating the ideas and resources of a diverse set of persons and organizations can appear initially daunting and impossible.

Just as the religious community cannot be characterized as wholly moral and upright, the business community cannot be seen as completely immoral and full of greed. Similarly, just as the nonprofit sector can be prone to ignoring the concerns of its clients (choosing instead to address the desires of certain donors and benefactors), the public sector reneges on its role of developing and implementing public policies and programs that are designed to meet the needs of the broader public (instead, responding to certain special or political interests). There are innumerable examples that effectively dispel any existing generalizations across the sectors and provide evidence that individuals and institutions from all sectors contribute to the good of humanity in many ways. It is simply unfair and unrealistic to expect all persons and organizations of an entire sector to adhere to the same principles and practices.

Our uniqueness and multiplicity as they relate to how we utilize limited resources and talents are what make us such a rich and diverse human community. Moreover, our diversity, particularly within each sector, highlights our unlimited potential for effecting positive changes in the lives of many people. One individual's or institution's expression or interpretation of serving humanity should not be hindered by another's narrow understanding of what it means to serve. There are no monoliths when it comes to meeting the needs of people; no one sector can claim a monopoly on or exclusive rights to the services required when responding to the economic, spiritual, social, and other complexities confronting people on a daily basis. My contention is that service to humanity will be fulfilled through a variety of forums across the nonprofit, private, public, and religious sectors.

From the United Nations to oil companies and environmental groups, collaboration across sectors has proven to be a viable option for resolving issues such as poverty, disease, and health care. Examples of professions and industries that are employing collaborative strategies include the medical and public health fields' developing strategic alliances to create comprehensive approaches to medical care; postsecondary institutions' partnering with local schools and national foundations to implement math and science programs; and private corporations' collaborating with universities to build bridges between theoretical and applied research. *A Call to the Village* can facilitate new communities of persons and organizations who combine their resources and responsibilities to improve public education in new and meaningful ways. Through the process of collaboration, these entities will educate and inform one another in ways that enable the fulfillment of our collective mandate, as well as the bridging of gaps (or gulfs) that have isolated us. Tradition should not be used as an excuse for doing nothing; rather, it should serve as an inspiration to do something of service in school-age education.